AS Law
UNIT 3

AQA

Module 3: The Concept of Liability

Ian Yule

Philip Allan Updates
Market Place
Deddington
Oxfordshire
OX15 0SE

Tel: 01869 338652
Fax: 01869 337590
e-mail: sales@philipallan.co.uk
www.philipallan.co.uk

© Philip Allan Updates 2003

ISBN 0 86003 933 1

This guide has been written specifically to support students preparing for the AQA AS Law Unit 3 examination. The content has been neither approved nor endorsed by AQA and remains the sole responsibility of the author.

Printed by Information Press, Eynsham, Oxford

P00171

Contents

Introduction

■ ■ ■

Content Guidance

■ ■ ■

Questions and Answers

Introduction

About this guide

The AQA specification for the AS and A2 Law examinations is divided into six modules. Unit 3 makes up the substantive, i.e. 'real law', element for AS; the legal topics covered are those of criminal liability and the tort law of negligence. Unlike the other two AS modules, which are assessed by essay-style examinations with a choice of questions, this module is assessed by compulsory 'problem-solving' questions.

You are presented with two brief 'scenarios'. The first one deals with some form of criminal attack where you are required to answer a general question on an issue relating to criminal liability and then identify from the scenario which particular offences may have been committed. The second scenario addresses the issue of the tort of negligence, and you need to be able to describe the three key elements of duty of care, breach of duty and remoteness of damage. The final question can be about either sentencing, concentrating on the types of different sentences available, or compensatory damages, dealing with the various 'heads' of damages.

There are three sections to this guide:

- **Introduction** — this provides advice on how this guide should be used, an explanation of the skills required to complete the unit successfully and guidance on revision techniques.
- **Content Guidance** — this sets out the specification content for Unit 3. It also contains references to cases which you will need to study for a sound understanding of each topic.
- **Questions and Answers** — this section provides 11 sample AS questions. All questions are followed by A- and C-grade answers. Examiner comments show how marks are awarded or why they are withheld. As this is a 'substantive' law module, it is even more important than in the other AS modules to be able to use case law effectively. The Question and Answer section gives some examples of how to employ case and statutory references to best effect.

How to use this guide

The Content Guidance covers all the elements of the Unit 3 specification, breaking it down into manageable sections for study and learning. It is not intended to be a comprehensive and detailed set of notes for the unit — the material needs to be supplemented by further reading from textbooks and case studies.

At the end of each section, make a summary of the factual material under the appropriate headings, incorporating additional material from your wider reading and research, and then test yourself by using the sample question(s) on that particular topic. By practising questions and assessing your answers against the examiner's comments you will learn how to use your knowledge and understanding effectively to improve your exam grade.

Learning strategies

It is essential to build up a good set of notes. These notes need to be laid out clearly under the headings used in the Content Guidance section. Your notes should contain accurate definitions and explanations together with relevant case and statutory references. It is also recommended that you compile summaries of the most important cases — this will make it much easier to remember these cases and to use them in examination answers.

Revision planning

At this level of study, it is essential that you understand the need to learn basic factual information thoroughly — this should be done as the module is being taught. Don't leave it to the revision stage, otherwise you will find that there is simply too much detailed knowledge to absorb.

Remember that the word 'revise' is defined in the *Concise Oxford Dictionary* as to 'read again (work learnt or done) to improve one's knowledge'. Skimming over some notes or reading this guide is *not* revision if you have not already learnt the material.

The first stage of revision requires organisation of all your work. Ensure that:
- your class notes are up to date
- you have used the material in this guide effectively
- you have made accurate notes on any wider reading, especially of case studies

The final key stage is the summarising of all the material, organised under the headings and subheadings within this unit specification. The revision period is the time to go over all the notes and reduce them to manageable proportions. This is, in itself, an effective learning exercise. The act of summarising makes it easier to recall the material and should reduce the chance of forgetting parts of it in the examination. The greatest number of exam marks are lost not through failure to understand the material, but simply through forgetting fuller explanations and, in this unit particularly, how to use relevant cases.

Assessment objectives

Assessment objectives (AOs) are common to AS and A2 units and are intended to assess candidates' ability to:
- recall, select, deploy and develop knowledge and understanding of legal principles accurately and by means of examples
- analyse legal material, issues and situations, and evaluate and apply the appropriate legal rules and principles
- present a logical and coherent argument and communicate relevant material in a clear and effective manner, using correct legal terminology

Examination technique

Case references

The importance of case references cannot be overemphasised. A 'case-free' answer rarely obtains more than a D or E grade, and will more often be awarded a U grade. Without appropriate case references, it is simply not possible to demonstrate a sound understanding of relevant law. Remember, the cases you have been taught do not just 'illustrate' that rule of law; in many cases they *are* the law. Remember also that the mark scheme often prevents examiners awarding marks if there is no reference to case or statutory authorities. There have been occasions when, although the content of an answer in terms of explanation could have merited a higher mark band, the absence of cases has meant that up to 2 marks have been lost for a 10-mark question.

Matching cases to the correct legal rule

Many candidates appear to believe that as long as some cases are mentioned, it does not matter too much if they are the right ones! Look carefully at the A- and C-grade answers in the Question and Answer section, and you will recognise the importance of using cases correctly. When revising, make a point of learning the correct case for each offence in terms of *actus reus* and *mens rea*, and for the separate rules in tort law.

Using cases

It is rarely necessary or desirable to describe the facts of the cases cited — the important part of a case is the legal rule it created or demonstrates. For example, poor examination technique would cite the case of *Donoghue* v *Stevenson* and simply retell the sad story of Mrs Donoghue and the snail in the bottle for up to half a side. This is a waste of time — what the examiner wants to see is a short and accurate explanation of the 'neighbour principle'. It is a good idea to make a brief reference to the facts, e.g. mentioning that this is the 'snail in the bottle case', or the 'Jehovah's Witness case', or the 'cricket ball case' etc. The only occasion when a more detailed description of the facts in a cited case is required is when the facts of the question scenario match them very closely. A good example of this occurred in the June 2002 examination, when the tort scenario question was clearly based on the case of *Smith* v *Leech Brain*.

Omissions

This is the greatest single source of lost marks. Try to remember series of facts or rules, for example the three tests for duty of care and the different questions used to establish the 'reasonable man' test in breach of duty of care. In comparing the A- and C-grade answers in the Question and Answer section, note the material which is omitted from the C-grade answers and the inadequate explanations.

QWC marks

There are 5 marks for each AS paper for quality of written communication (10 marks for each A2 paper). The easiest way to lose some of these is to misspell basic legal words such as *grievous, defendant, deterrence, assault, sentence*. Finally, check your spelling, use paragraphs correctly and make your handwriting as clear as possible.

Planning your answers effectively

When you look at the A-grade answers you will recognise immediately that there is a clear structure to each of these, usually demonstrated straight away by a simple, accurate and relevant first sentence. The C-grade answers lack this element of planning and structure. You should read the question carefully and make sure you understand what it is asking, and then make a short plan — it could be in the form of a spider diagram or just a series of headings and subheadings. After this, read the question again to check that your plan is both relevant and accurate. Don't worry about how to introduce your answers — this is not an English exam. Look carefully at how the A-grade answers start and model your own technique on these.

Time planning

Contrary to popular belief, few students have a problem with lack of time in the examination. By doing homework essays and timed or practice examination essays you will learn whether you are a quick or a slow writer, and whether you are likely to experience time difficulties. If you feel there is likely to be a time problem, note that this makes planning even more vital. There is no point in wasting time on material which is either inaccurate or irrelevant.

Those who finish early — and this will apply to most candidates — should first check their answers to ensure that key legal rules and appropriate cases have been included. Next they should look at their plans to ensure they have covered all the points. If at the end of this process there is still time left, they should consider what additional material can quickly be added, such as an additional case or, in an s.20 GBH/wounding answer, a short reference to s.18, some extra details on a type of sentence or head of damages, and so on. In the majority of exam scripts, it would be possible to improve the overall result by almost one grade (which can be as little as 1 or 2 marks) by adding such material.

Notice from the A-grade answers in this book the amount of material required for such a grade — note also the fact that C-grade answers are very often significantly *longer* than those that achieve a grade A.

Module 3 revision checklist

Criminal law	*Actus reus*, omission, and relevant cases
	Causation rules and cases
	Mens rea, intention (direct and oblique) and cases
	Recklessness
	Coincidence of *actus reus* and *mens rea*
	Transferred malice
	Strict liability offences — cases

Non-fatal offences	Assault
	Battery
	S.47 ABH: *actus reus* and *mens rea*, and cases
	S.20 wounding/infliction of GBH: *actus reus* and *mens rea*, and cases
	S.18 *mens rea* elements
	Joint Charging Standard — details of qualifying injuries for each offence
Tort of negligence	Duty of care: 'neighbourhood' test, *Caparo Industries plc* v *Dickman*. Proximity and 'just, fair and reasonable' test
	Breach of duty: 'reasonable man' and illustrative tests and cases
	Remoteness of damage: 'but for' test, Wagon Mound case, 'thin skull' test and relevant cases
Damages	Purpose of damages
	Compensatory and non-compensatory damages
	General damages, especially loss of future earnings
	Special damages
	Relevant cases and statutes
Sentencing	Aims of sentences: retribution, deterrence, rehabilitation and protection of society
	Types of sentences: custodial, community, financial and discharge
	Aggravating and mitigating factors

Summary of main legal terms used in this guide

Actus reus

Actus reus is the physical element required for criminal liability which can comprise an act, an omission or a state of affairs. It has to be the voluntary, controlled act of the defendant. Key terms for the concept of *actus reus* are:

omission: the failure to act in circumstances where the law imposes a duty to do so. Examples include where the defendant has created a dangerous situation (*R* v *Miller*), where the defendant has assumed a responsibility (*R* v *Stone and Dobinson*), or where the defendant's contract of employment requires him or her to act in the interests of the safety of others (*R* v *Pitwood*).

causation: the legal rule which requires the prosecution to prove that the defendant was 'the cause' of the prohibited consequence. Two rules are the factual 'but for' rule (*R* v *White*), and the legal rule that the defendant must have made 'a significant contribution' to the unlawful outcome (*R* v *Cheshire*).

Mens rea

Mens rea is the mental element of criminal liability which can be intention, recklessness or gross negligence (which you don't need to know about in any detail for Unit 3):

intention: this can be **direct**, where it is the defendant's aim, purpose or objective to achieve the unlawful result. In other cases, it can be **oblique**, where defendants can argue that although they caused the unlawful outcome, they did so in circumstances where that was not their intention. This requires the jury to consider the elements of probability and foreseeability. The leading cases are those of *R* v *Nedrick* and *R* v *Woollin*, which created the rule of 'foresight of virtually certain consequences'.

recklessness: for all non-fatal offences, this is 'Cunningham' or 'subjective' recklessness — the conscious taking of an unjustified risk. This means the prosecution must prove that the defendant recognised the risk which was being taken.

transferred malice: the rule that if A intends to shoot and kill B but misses and kills C, the 'intention' aimed at B is transferred to C, and A is guilty in these circumstances of C's murder.

coincidence of *actus reus* **and** *mens rea:* this rule requires these elements to occur together. Note the 'continuing act' or 'linked transactions' rule from the cases of *R* v *Thabo Meli* and *Fagan* v *Metropolitan Police Commissioner*.

strict liability offences: these require no *mens rea* to be proved — they are 'no fault' crimes. Examples include many road traffic offences and breaches of pollution or work safety laws.

Tort of negligence

Tort of negligence is an actionable wrong which flows from a breach of duty of care that causes a victim foreseeable harm or loss. The key elements which the claimant needs to prove are that:

- he or she was owed a duty of care by the defendant
- the defendant breached that duty, and
- the breach caused the claimant foreseeable harm or loss

duty of care: this is a legal test which is based on the 'neighbour' test from *Donoghue* v *Stevenson* or the three-stage test from *Caparo Industries plc* v *Dickman*. Key factors examined are foreseeability of harm, proximity (closeness in terms of time, space and relationship) and the policy issue as to whether it is 'just, fair and reasonable' to impose a duty of care.

breach of duty: here the test is whether the defendant acted in the way 'reasonable man' would have done. The law takes into account factors such as probability of harm (*Bolton* v *Stone*), the magnitude or seriousness of that harm (*Paris* v *Stepney Borough Council*), together with the cost and practicality of taking precautions (*Latimer* v *AEB*).

remoteness of damage: this final test examines whether the defendant's actions or omissions caused the harm and, if so, whether that harm or loss was a reasonably foreseeable consequence of the defendant's action or omission — as in the *Wagon Mound* case.

Sentencing

Sentencing is the imposition of a penalty following the conviction of the defendant. The aims of sentencing are:

retribution: punishment 'which fits the crime' and gives the defendant his or her 'just deserts', i.e. confirms that the punishment is deserved for the crime committed.

deterrence: this can be either individual (to seek to prevent the particular defendant from reoffending) or general (to discourage the general public from committing crimes).

rehabilitation or reform: this aims to address the cause of the defendant's criminality and thereby to 'reform' him or her through education, drug treatment etc.

protection of society: the court will impose a custodial sentence on violent or sexual criminals to ensure that they cannot reoffend for some time. Serious violent or sexual offenders now receive much longer sentences of imprisonment than was once the case.

Types of sentence include:

custodial: imprisonment or youth custody — these may be imposed only if the offence committed is sufficiently serious.

community: non-custodial sentence involving the offender's supervision in the community under a community rehabilitation order (formerly probation) or a community punishment order.

financial: fines or compensation orders.

discharge: absolute or conditional.

Aggravating and mitigating factors are considered by the trial judge in order to 'fine tune' the sentence imposed on the defendant. Their effects are as follows:

aggravating factors will result in a heavier sentence being imposed. They include factors such as use of a weapon, a defendant's lack of remorse for the crime, the special vulnerability of the victim, or breach of trust.

mitigating factors will result in the imposition of a less severe sentence — either a community sentence or a shorter custodial sentence. Examples of mitigating factors include a plea of guilty, an offer by the defendant to compensate the victim, or the fact that it is a first offence.

Damages

The purpose of damages in tort law is primarily to compensate victims by restoring them to the position they would have been in had the tort not occurred. The main 'heads' of damages are special and general damages.

special damages: these are quantifiable losses between the tort and the trial which include medical expenses and loss of earnings.

general damages: these include all other losses, especially future loss of earnings, compensation for pain and suffering, and loss of amenity.

Content Guidance

The specification for Unit 3 outlined in this section is as follows:

Introduction to criminal liability

Actus reus
- Crimes of omission
- Rules of causation

Mens rea
- Introduction and general explanation
- Intention
- Recklessness
- Coincidence of *actus reus* and *mens rea*
- Transferred malice
- Strict liability offences

Non-fatal offences
- Assault
- Battery
- S.47 assault occasioning actual bodily harm
- S.20 malicious wounding or inflicting grievous bodily harm
- S.18 wounding or causing grievous bodily harm with intent (to cause GBH)
- Summary of non-fatal offences
- Joint Charging Standard

Tort law
- Introduction
- Duty of care
- Breach of duty of care
- Causation of foreseeable loss or injury

Damages
- Special damages
- General damages
- Provisional damages
- Structured settlements
- Death of the victim

Sentencing
- Aims of sentencing
- Types of sentence
- Mitigating and aggravating factors
- Maximum sentences

In this unit, all the questions are compulsory. This means that all the elements in the specification need to be learnt.

Introduction to criminal liability

The traditional basis for criminal liability — that is liability to be prosecuted in a criminal court and, if convicted, to be punished by the state — is an *actus reus*, the physical element, accompanied by the appropriate *mens rea*, the mental element. In this section, these are the two areas which need to be looked at in some detail.

It is a general principle of criminal law that a person may not be convicted of a crime unless the prosecution has proved beyond doubt both (a) that he or she has caused a certain event or that responsibility is to be attributed to him or her for the existence of a certain state of affairs, which is forbidden by criminal law, and (b) that he or she had a defined state of mind in relation to the event or state of affairs. The event or state of affairs is called the *actus reus* and the state of mind the *mens rea* of the crime.

Actus literally means 'act', but while most crimes involve the accused committing a certain act, this is not always the case. Criminal liability may also arise through a failure to act (an omission) and from a certain type of conduct. *Actus reus* means literally 'prohibited act', but few crimes can be adequately described simply by reference to the act; most require proof of accompanying circumstances and some proof of a particular consequence. For example, in criminal damage the offence consists of destroying or damaging property which belongs to another (the act), and for there to be no lawful excuse (the circumstances).

Each separate crime has its own specific *actus reus* — for battery it is the infliction of unlawful personal violence. For assault occasioning actual bodily harm, it is both the original assault or (more usually) battery and the actual bodily harm suffered by the victim as a consequence.

Note also that while *mens rea* may exist without an *actus reus*, if the *actus reus* of a particular crime does not exist or occur, that crime is not committed.

Actus reus

Ordinarily the prosecution must prove that the accused person voluntarily brought about the *actus reus* of the crime, i.e. the act or omission must have occurred because of a conscious exercise of will of the defendant. If in an assault case the defendant's arm was physically forced by another to strike the victim, or if the defendant was pushed against the victim by another, then there would be no crime by the defendant, although it is probable that the perpetrator of the force would be guilty of crimes against both the defendant and the victim.

Crimes of omission

As well as actions such as hitting someone over the head or stealing a wallet, an *actus reus* can also be an omission or failure to act. In most criminal prosecutions the prosecutor will be seeking to prove that a prohibited situation or result has been brought about by the acts of the defendant. However, in certain situations it will be the fact that the defendant failed to act that led to the prohibited event occurring.

Most jurisdictions, including that of England and Wales, have not adopted a general principle of liability for failing to act. Instead, the law has defined certain factual situations in which persons shall be under a duty to act, and, if they fail to act in these situations, thereby causing a prohibited criminal result, they shall be liable for that result.

There are six areas where such liability for omissions exists:

(1) Where there is a contractual duty to act. In *R v Pittwood,* a railway crossing gatekeeper opened the gate to let a cart through and went off to lunch, forgetting to shut it again. Ten minutes later a haycart, while crossing the line, was struck by a train and the driver was killed. The gatekeeper was convicted of manslaughter on the ground that 'there was gross and criminal negligence, as the man was paid to keep the gate shut and protect the public...A man may incur criminal liability from a duty arising out of contract'.

(2) Statute can make it an offence in defined circumstances to fail to act — see s.1(1) of the **Children and Young Persons Act 1933**. The House of Lords ruled that the *actus reus* of the offence is simply the failure for whatever reason to provide the child with the necessary medical care.

(3) One can be made liable where there is an assumed responsibility for the care of an aged or infirm person, as in the case of *R v Stone and Dobinson* where an unmarried cohabiting couple invited Stone's middle-aged sister, who was anorexic, to come and live with them. Although Stone and Dobinson were aware that the woman was neglecting herself and was deteriorating rapidly, they did nothing to assist her or to summon medical help or to inform social services. Three years after she came to live with them, she was found dead in her bed, naked and severely emaciated. The cause of death was toxaemia from the infected bed sores and prolonged immobilisation. Stone and Dobinson were convicted of her manslaughter — they had assumed a duty of care for her, a duty which they could easily have discharged by calling for help or by providing even basic care.

(4) Statute can make certain omissions an offence, such as failure to wear a seat belt or to stop after a road accident and report it.

(5) Liability also exists where the defendant has by his or her own acts created a dangerous situation — see *R v Miller.* In this case, Lord Diplock had no doubts that the defendant had been convicted correctly. This was because the *actus reus* of the offence of arson is present if the defendant accidentally starts a fire and fails to take any steps to extinguish it or prevent damage due to an intention to destroy or damage property belonging to another or being reckless whether any such property would be destroyed or damaged (as in this case). The defendant by his own admission became aware of the fire and chose to do nothing; this case is *not* suggesting liability for purely accidental fire. It should be noted here that, if, when Miller realised he had started a fire, he had tried to phone for the fire brigade or had alerted neighbours, he would not have incurred criminal liability even if in the meantime the fire had spread to an adjoining gas-holder and half the town had blown up!

(6) A defendant may have a particular occupation which requires him or her to act in such a way to protect other people — see *R* v *Dytham*. In this instance, a police officer was held guilty of a crime when, without justification, he failed to perform his duty to preserve the Queen's Peace by not protecting a citizen who was being kicked to death.

In most of these rules a case is used to show an example of the type of omission that results in a defendant being convicted of a crime. It is essential that you learn these cases — this is one of the key points which examiners are looking for.

The most common examples of omissions in exam questions are those of 'assumed responsibility', where a relative or other responsible adult takes on responsibility for the care of a child, and the *R* v *Miller* 'dangerous situation', where the defendant has accidentally 'created a dangerous situation' and has thus simultaneously put himself or herself under a duty of care to do something about it.

Rules of causation

Another issue that needs to be understood is that of causation. This occurs in so-called 'result' crimes — those that need an act which then goes on to cause a specific result. In murder, for example, to be guilty the defendant must not only have attacked the victim in some way but must also have caused the victim to die.

The 'but for' rule

The first rule to be considered is the factual rule of causation, referred to as the 'but for' rule, which simply requires the prosecution to prove that 'but for' the defendant's act, the event would not have occurred. This is well illustrated by the famous case of *R* v *White*, where the defendant put potassium cyanide into a drink called 'nectar' with intent to murder his mother. She was found dead shortly afterwards with the glass, three parts filled, beside her. The medical evidence showed that she had died not of poisoning, but of heart failure. The defendant was acquitted of murder and convicted of attempted murder. Although the consequence which the defendant intended had occurred, he did not cause it to occur and therefore there was no *actus reus* of murder.

While it is usually very easy to prove this 'but for' rule, there are many situations where the question of causation is much more difficult to establish clearly. A. M. Dugdale in *A Level Law* (Butterworths, 3rd edn, 1996) lists some examples:

- A points a gun at B and B dies of a heart attack.

- A knocks B unconscious and leaves him lying in a road, where he is run over by a car and killed.
- A injures B, who is being taken by ambulance to the hospital when the ambulance crashes, killing all the occupants.
- A knocks B unconscious and she remains lying in a street for several hours, where she is robbed, raped or assaulted further.

In all the above examples, it could be argued that A caused the consequences on the basis that none of these events would have happened 'but for' the initial attack by A on B. The obvious difficulty with this approach, however, is that it can link an initial cause (the attack) with consequences which are both highly improbable and unforeseeable. This has been a particular problem in cases of unlawful killing — murder and manslaughter — where there is a less direct link between act and effect. In such cases one has to consider what the responsibility of the defendant is for the victim's death. At one time the legal position was that the defendant was liable for all natural and probable consequences of his or her voluntary acts, but this presumption has now been overturned on the grounds that this formula could link together events that are too remotely connected. In *R v Marjoram* the trial judge instructed the jury to consider the legal cause — there must be something which could reasonably be foreseen as a consequence of the unlawful act. Nowadays it is accepted law that the defendant need only have made 'a significant contribution' to the unlawful result, as in *R v Cheshire* (1991), or have been an 'operative and substantial cause of harm'.

Another good case exemplifying this principle is *R v Smith* (1959), where a fight between two soldiers resulted in the victim receiving a bayonet wound requiring medical treatment. While being carried to the medical reception station, the victim was dropped twice. The doctor failed to diagnose a punctured lung and gave treatment which was later described as 'thoroughly bad'. Smith was convicted of murder and his appeal failed. The key rule was that: 'if at the time of death the original wound is still the operating and substantial cause, then the death can properly be said to be the result of the wound, albeit some other cause of death is also operating. Only if it can be said that the original wound is merely the setting in which another cause operates can it be said that the death does not result from the wound.' This situation occurred in the case of *R v Jordan*, where the victim of a serious injury made a good recovery in hospital but while recuperating received an injection of a drug to which he was allergic. The doctors confirmed that the death was not caused by the original wound, which was mainly healed at the time of death, but by the injection (and also the intravenous introduction of large quantities of liquid).

Further rules that occur in causation address the question of what constitutes a new intervening act (*novus actus interveniens*) — this requires something which cannot be foreseen, and it must be so overwhelming as to invalidate the original *actus reus*. For example, A shoots at B and causes B serious internal injuries which could be treated successfully if immediate and specialised medical treatment were provided, but the ambulance takes 10 minutes to arrive and as a result B dies. This is a foreseeable result and A is guilty of murder. Also note what are called 'escape cases', in which the victim has suffered injury or has been killed while trying to escape from a serious attack. In such cases, the defendant will be liable if the victim's conduct in running away was within the range of foreseeable responses to the defendant's behaviour.

The 'thin skull' rule

The 'thin skull' rule or 'take your victim as you find him' refers to the situation where the intervening cause is a pre-existing weakness of the victim, for instance an abnormally thin skull. If, because of this, a blow inflicted on the victim causes serious injury or even death, when in a 'normal' person it would usually only cause a bruise, the attacker is liable for the more serious injury or the death. This rule covers not only physical but mental conditions, and even the victim's beliefs or values, as in *R v Blaue*. Here the victim of a stabbing was a Jehovah's Witness, who refused on religious grounds to accept a blood transfusion which would have saved her life. The defendant was convicted of her manslaughter and the Court of Appeal rejected his appeal, holding that the victim's refusal to accept the transfusion did not break the causal chain.

In most of the questions that are likely to be asked in this unit, this issue should not present too many difficulties, but remember that these rules are even more important if you study fatal offences in Unit 4.

Mens rea

Having looked at issues of *actus reus* — the physical element in a crime — we now need to examine the even more important areas dealt with under *mens rea* — the mental element necessary for all serious crimes. Criminal law does not exist to punish a person who has committed some kind of wrongful action; to be criminally liable, that person must have done that wrongful act in circumstances in which blame can be attached to his or her conduct. To put it more simply, a criminal is punished not so much on account of what he or she has done but because of why he or she did it. All the crimes which form part of this module — non-fatal offences, and those which are included in later A2 modules — have both a separate *actus reus* and *mens rea*. The following states of mind are used to denote *mens rea*:

- intention — where the offender has made a decision to break the law
- recklessness — which applies to those who act while realising that there is a possibility that their action could cause the illegal outcome
- gross negligence — which covers those situations where the defendant did not foresee causing any harm, but should have realised the risks involved. An example is the case where an anaesthetist failed to recognise and deal with the problems which arose when the breathing tube slipped out of a patient's mouth. As a result the patient died during the operation.

For the crimes studied in this module, it is enough that we examine the issues surrounding intention and recklessness. All these offences — except 'wounding or causing grievous bodily harm with intent' — can be committed either intentionally or recklessly.

Intention

The meaning of intention is not to be found in any statute; its meaning is to be found in judicial decisions. It is clear that a person intends a result when it is his or her aim or objective or purpose to bring it about. This might be termed 'dictionary intention'.

However, the concept of intention is open to ambiguity. What is the position when someone has clearly caused an illegal result, realising that it would almost certainly occur, although it was not his or her primary intention? There is a well-known hypothetical example of a person placing a bomb in an aircraft with the intention that it will explode when the plane reaches an altitude of 20,000 feet. His specific aim or objective is to obtain the insurance money on the lost aircraft. In these circumstances he surely knows that when the plane explodes all the passengers and crew will be killed, but does he really intend their deaths? This type of case is called one of **oblique intent**.

In the case of *R* v *Hancock and Shankland*, this issue was at the heart of the case — how the law should deal with the defendant who has created an unlawful result where it is clear that the outcome was probable, even highly probable, and the defendant may well have foreseen this outcome. The defendants in the case were Welsh coal miners on strike. When one of their fellow miners wanted to return to work, they tried to stop the strike-breaker as he was being driven to another coal mine in a taxi. The route took the miners onto a motorway. When the taxi passed under a bridge, the striking miners threw rocks from the bridge. One of the larger rocks smashed through the windscreen and killed the driver. Clearly the defendants had killed the taxi driver and had they been charged with manslaughter would have pleaded guilty. However, the charge was murder, which requires there to be intention to kill or commit serious injury. The defendants denied such an intention, admitting only that their intention was to prevent the strike-breaker reaching the coal mine.

Although they were convicted of murder at their trial, the Court of Appeal and the House of Lords both quashed that conviction and substituted a manslaughter conviction, holding that the issue of intention had not been established. Lord Scarman indicated that, in cases like these, juries needed to be told by the judge that 'the greater the probability of a consequence occurring, the more likely it was so foreseen and, if so, the more likely it was intended'. This emphasised the point that foresight of the degree of probability was the only evidence from which intention could be inferred.

In the more recent cases of *R* v *Nedrick* and *R* v *Woollin* (see below), a tighter rule was laid down for such cases of oblique intent. This now requires juries to return a verdict of murder only where they find that 'the defendant foresaw death or serious injury as a virtually certain consequence of his or her voluntary actions'. It is worth pointing out that in both these cases, the original murder conviction was changed on appeal to a manslaughter conviction.

R v *Woollin* (1998)

This case resulted from the death of a 3-month-old baby. Although initially the defendant gave a number of different explanations, he finally admitted that he 'had lost his cool' when his baby started to choke. He had shaken the baby and then, in a fit of rage or frustration, had thrown him in the direction of his pram which was standing against the wall some 3 or 4 feet away. He knew that the baby's head had hit something hard but denied intending to throw him against the wall or wanting him to die or to suffer serious injury. The trial judge directed the members of jury that they might infer intention if they were satisfied that when he threw the baby, the defendant appreciated there was a 'substantial risk' of causing serious harm. In the Court of Appeal, the defendant argued that the judge should have used the words 'virtual certainty', as 'substantial risk' was merely a test of recklessness. The Court of Appeal, although critical of the trial judge, dismissed the appeal, and certified questions for the House of Lords. The House of Lords quashed the defendant's conviction for murder and substituted a conviction for manslaughter.

Lord Steyn gave the main speech, saying that 'a result foreseen as virtually certain is an intended result'. Thus the phrase 'substantial risk' used by the trial judge blurred the distinction between intention and recklessness, and was too serious a misdirection for the conviction to stand.

Recklessness

A standard dictionary definition of this is 'unjustified risk-taking'; English law has complicated the matter by distinguishing two different kinds of recklessness named after two cases, Cunningham recklessness and Caldwell reckless.

Cunningham recklessness, also called 'subjective' recklessness

Here the prosecution must prove that the defendant appreciated that his or her action created an unjustified risk, and then went ahead with the action anyway. In the Cunningham case, the defendant ripped a gas meter from a wall to steal the money it contained, causing gas to escape. The gas seeped into a neighbouring building, where it overcame a woman. Cunningham was convicted of an s.23 offence — administering a noxious substance — but he appealed successfully on the ground that the prosecution had failed to prove that he recognised the risk of the gas escape. The question was quite simply whether the defendant *had* foreseen that his act might injure someone, not whether he *ought* to have foreseen this risk.

Caldwell recklessness, also called 'objective' recklessness

Here all that has to be proved is that the risk was so obvious that a reasonable person would have seen it. As Caldwell recklessness is now used only in criminal damage offences, it is not necessary for students to refer to Caldwell recklessness within a non-fatal offence question. It usually serves only to create confusion.

Coincidence of actus reus and mens rea

Mens rea must coincide in point of time with the *actus reus*. If I happen to kill my neighbour accidentally, I do not become a murderer by thereafter expressing joy over his death, even if a week previously I had planned to kill him but had then changed my mind. *Mens rea* implies an intention to do a present act, not a future one. In most cases, there is no problem in proving the necessary coincidence of *actus reus* and *mens rea*, but there are a few cases which illustrate the fact that judges can take a more generous view of this issue of coincidence.

One such case is that of Thabo Meli, where the defendants clearly intended to kill their victim and, having attacked him severely, threw what they believed to be his dead body over a cliff in order to dispose of it. The victim in fact survived both the murderous attack and the fall, and died subsequently of exposure. On appeal, the Privy Council ruled that it was 'impossible to divide up what was really one series of acts' and that, if, during that series of acts, the necessary *mens rea* was present, that was sufficient coincidence to justify a conviction. This ruling was followed in *R v Church*. A more recent case was *R v Le Brun*, where again the view was upheld that where there is series of actions which can be regarded as a linked transaction or continuing act, provided that at some point during the transaction the required *mens rea* is present, the coincidence rule is satisfied.

A final example is that of *Fagan v Metropolitan Police Commissioner*. Here the facts were that the defendant had accidentally driven his car onto a police officer's foot when he had been instructed to park his car close to the kerb. When the officer ordered him to move it, Fagan swore and turned off the ignition. When he was later convicted of assaulting a police officer in the execution of his duty, Fagan appealed on the ground that when he drove accidentally onto the officer's foot there was no *mens rea* and when he had *mens rea* (when he swore and turned off the ignition) there was no act but an omission (failure to act), and the *actus reus* of this particular crime required an act. The appeal was dismissed — the court held that Fagan's driving onto the officer's foot and staying there was one single continuous act rather than an act followed by an omission. So long as the defendant had the *mens rea* at some point during that continuous act, he was liable.

Another relevant issue to consider here is that of strict liability offences, where there is no need to prove *mens rea*.

Transferred malice

Under the rule of 'transferred malice', if A fires a gun at B, intending to kill B, but misses and in fact kills C, A is guilty of murdering C. The intention (malice) is transferred from B to C. The leading case is that of *R v Latimer*. In this case, the defendant had a quarrel in a public house with another person. He took off his belt and aimed a blow at his intended victim which struck him lightly. However, the belt then struck a person standing beside the intended victim and wounded her severely. The jury found that the blow was unlawfully aimed at the original victim but that the striking of the second victim was purely accidental. It was held on appeal, however, that the defendant should be convicted of unlawfully and maliciously wounding the second victim.

The other important aspect of this rule is that it is limited to situations where the *actus reus* and the *mens rea* of the same crime coincide. If A shoots at B's dog, intending to kill it, but misses and instead kills B, A is not guilty of B's murder because the *mens rea* of murder is not present.

Strict liability offences

Strict liability offences may be defined as those which do not require *mens rea* to be proved. Another way of describing these is to call them 'no fault' offences, and almost all of them are created by statute law. Many of them concern road traffic offences or breaches of health and safety legislation.

A good example of such a crime is that in *R* v *Prince*, which involved the unlawful abduction of a 13-year-old girl. The jury found that there was reasonable evidence that she had told the defendant before the abduction that she was 18, and that he genuinely believed her. However, the court held that the relevant statute could be interpreted as allowing strict liability, and the fact that the defendant did not know that the girl was under 16 was irrelevant as no *mens rea* was required for the offence. It is also clear from this case that a mistake about the strict liability element, here the age of the child, is irrelevant, even if that mistake is a reasonable one.

The argument most frequently advanced by the courts for imposing strict liability is that it is necessary to do so in the interests of the public. It may be conceded that, in many of the instances where strict liability has been imposed, the public does need protection against negligence and, assuming that the threat of punishment can make the potential harmdoer more careful, there may be a valid ground for imposing liability for negligence as well as where there is *mens rea*. This is particularly true when the offence involves a non-human consequence such as causing pollution; the courts have consistently ruled that such an offence is one of strict liability. A good illustrative case is *Alphacell* v *Woodward*, where the House of Lords held that the offence of causing polluted matter to enter a river was a strict liability offence.

It is also argued that the majority of strict liability cases can be described as 'administrative' or 'quasi' crimes. Parliament makes no such distinction: an act either is, or is not, declared by Parliament to be a crime, but the courts decide whether it is a 'real' or 'quasi' crime on the basis that an offence which, in the public eye, carries little or no stigma and does not involve 'the disgrace of criminality' is only a 'quasi' crime. Then strict liability may be imposed, because 'it does not offend the ordinary man's sense of justice that moral guilt is not of the essence of the offence'. In *Sweet* v *Parsley* this distinction had previously been made. Here Lord Reid acknowledged that strict liability was appropriate for regulatory offences, or 'quasi' crimes — offences which are not criminal 'in any real sense', and are merely acts prohibited in the public interest. But, he said, the kind of crime to which a real social stigma is attached should usually require proof of *mens rea*. In this case, the defendant's conviction for being concerned in the management of premises which were being used for the purpose of smoking cannabis was quashed on appeal on the ground that such an offence was not one of strict liability and did require *mens rea* to be proved.

A further point here is that, in most of these cases, the penalty imposed is a fine and not a community or custodial sentence. However, in *Gammon* v *Attorney-General of Hong Kong*, the Privy Council admitted that the fact that the offence was punishable with a fine of $250,000 and 3 years' imprisonment was not inconsistent with the imposition of strict liability.

Non-fatal offences

Now that you have studied the 'theory' in terms of *actus reus* and *mens rea*, you can apply it to actual offences — those grouped together as non-fatal offences. There are five of these:

- assault
- battery
- assault occasioning actual bodily harm (ABH)
- malicious wounding or inflicting grievous bodily harm (GBH)
- wounding or inflicting grievous bodily harm with intent (to cause GBH)

Assault and battery were two distinct crimes at common law and their separate existence is confirmed by s.39 of the **Criminal Justice Act 1988**. The other three more serious offences are defined in the **Offences Against the Person Act 1861.**

Assault

This is any act by which the defendant, intentionally or recklessly, causes the victim to apprehend immediate and unlawful personal violence. In other words, this offence can be described as 'a threat of violence which the victim believes to be a threat'. Accordingly, if any harm is caused, a more serious offence than assault has been committed, although the defendant may also have committed an assault, for example if the defendant has shouted at the victim 'I am going to thump you' and has then proceeded to do just that.

Actus reus of assault

In a typical case of an assault (as opposed to a battery), the defendant, by some physical movement, causes the victim to believe that he or she is about to be struck. There may even be an assault where the defendant has no intention to commit a battery but only to cause the victim to apprehend one. There is a tendency to enlarge the concept of assault by taking a generous view of 'immediacy', to include threats in which the impending impact is more remote. In *Logdon* v *DPP* it was held that the defendant committed an assault by showing his victim a pistol in a drawer and declaring that he would hold her hostage.

In *Smith* v *Superintendent of Woking Police*, the defendant committed an assault by looking at the victim in her night-clothes through a window, intending to frighten her. It was made clear in *R* v *Ireland* that an assault may be committed by words alone, or even, as in that case, by silent telephone calls where the caller 'intends by his silence to cause fear and he is so understood'.

There may be an assault even where the defendant has no means of carrying out the threat. The issue to be decided in these cases is whether the defendant intends to cause the victim to believe that he or she can and will carry it out, and whether the victim does so believe. It is clear that a threat to inflict harm at some future time cannot amount to an assault — an apprehension of immediate personal violence is essential. In *R* v *Constanza* it was held that there had been an assault when the victim read the letters which had been sent by a stalker and interpreted them as clear threats — there was a 'fear of violence at some time not excluding the immediate future'.

Battery

This is defined as 'any act by which the defendant, intentionally or recklessly, inflicts unlawful personal violence'. Most batteries involve an assault, and the tendency is to refer generically to 'assaults'. Examples of battery include a push, a kiss, or throwing a projectile or water which lands on another's body. Note that the battery need not be hostile or aggressive or rude. Many unwanted touchings are 'technical' batteries, and prosecutors are relied upon to avoid prosecutions of minor incidents. Since the merest touching without consent is a criminal offence, the demands of everyday life require that there be an implied consent to that degree of contact which is necessary or customary in ordinary life.

Actus reus of battery

This consists of the infliction of unlawful personal violence by the defendant. The use of the term 'violence' here is misleading — all that is required for a battery is that the defendant touch the victim without consent or other lawful excuse. However, under the Joint Charging Standard, in practice a prosecution is most unlikely unless some injury has been caused. It is generally said that the defendant must have carried out an act, but there can be occasions where mere obstruction can be a battery. There may also be a battery when the defendant inadvertently applies force to the victim and then wrongfully refuses to withdraw it. In *Fagan* v *Metropolitan Police Commissioner*, where the defendant accidentally drove his car onto a police officer's foot and then intentionally left it there, the court held that there was a continuing act, not a mere omission. It is also settled law that there can be a battery where there has been no direct contact with the victim's body — touching his or her clothing may be enough to constitute this offence, as in *R* v *Thomas*, where it was stated that touching the woman's skirt was equivalent to touching the woman herself.

Mens rea of assault and battery

The law is settled that either intention or recklessness as to the respective elements is sufficient. After a brief period of uncertainty, it is now clear that subjective reckless-ness — 'the conscious taking of an unjustified risk' — not Caldwell recklessness, is the relevant test (see the cases of *R* v *Venna*, *R* v *Savage*, *R* v *Parmenter*). The defendant must foresee the risk of causing apprehension of violence, or the application of violence, whichever the case may be.

Assault occasioning actual bodily harm (s.47)

Here the word 'assault' can mean either assault or battery, but most often it will refer to battery, the infliction of some unlawful violence rather than a threat of violence.

This offence is triable either way and carries a maximum sentence of 5 years' impris-onment — compare the maximum sentence of 6 months for common assault. The conduct element (*actus reus*) is an assault or battery which causes 'actual bodily harm'. This has been given the wide definition of 'any hurt or injury calculated to interfere with the health or comfort of the victim', provided it is not 'merely transient or trifling' — see *R* v *Miller*.

One consequence of this definition is that it has been held to cover psychological harm — where the defendant causes the victim to become hysterical or to suffer substantial fear (see *R* v *Chan-Fook*). Note, however, that in *R* v *Morris* the Court of Appeal held that evidence from the victim's doctor that she suffered from anxiety, fear, tearfulness, sleeplessness and physical tension was insufficient to establish actual bodily harm.

The *mens rea* required for this offence is the same as for battery — intention or recklessness as to the application of some unlawful force to another. This important rule was established in the separate cases of *Savage* and *Parmenter* where it was held by the House of Lords that the prosecution is not obliged for an s.47 offence to prove that the defendant intended to cause some actual bodily harm or was reckless as to whether such harm would be caused.

In *Savage*, the defendant admitted throwing the contents of her beer glass over the victim during a bar brawl. The glass slipped out of her hand and broke and a piece of glass cut the victim's wrist. This means that a verdict of guilty may be returned upon proof of an assault together with proof of the fact that actual bodily harm was occasioned by the assault. This is a key legal point that examiners are looking for. Students must note that this is one of the most common mistakes made in exami-nation answers. Few marks are awarded for referring to the *mens rea* of s.47 actual bodily harm as intention or recklessness unless there is a clear reference to this issue and these cases.

R v *Roberts* confirms that the *mens rea* of s.47 actual bodily harm is the same as for assault or battery. In this case, the defendant gave a lift in his car to a girl. During the journey he made unwanted sexual advances, touching the girl's clothes. Frightened that he was going to rape her, she jumped out of the moving car, injuring herself. It was held that the defendant had committed the *actus reus* of s.47 by touching her clothes — sufficient for battery — and this act had caused her to suffer actual bodily harm. The defendant argued that he lacked the *mens rea* of the offence, because he had neither intended to cause her actual bodily harm, nor seen any risk of her suffering it as a result of his advances. This argument was rejected: the court held that the *mens rea* of battery was sufficient in itself, and there was no need for any extra *mens rea* regarding the actual bodily harm.

Malicious wounding or inflicting grievous bodily harm (s.20)

This section created the offence of unlawfully and maliciously wounding or inflicting grievous bodily harm. The conduct element here is the same as for the more serious offence under s.18 (see below). A wound is defined as an injury which breaks both the outer and inner skin; a bruise or a burst blood vessel in the eye would not amount to a wound — see *C (a minor)* v *Eisenhower*. Grievous bodily harm is simply defined as 'really serious harm' — see *DPP* v *Smith* — or more simply as 'serious harm', see *R* v *Saunders*. Students should note that under the Joint Charging Standards, minor cuts would be charged as s.47 actual bodily harm, or even as battery.

The main difference between sections 18 and 20 lies in the fault element, and it is a considerable difference. Section 20 requires either intention or recklessness to inflict some harm. This fault element was confirmed in the cases of *R* v *Mowatt* and *R* v *Grimshaw*, which held that there is no need to prove recklessness as to wounding or grievous bodily harm, so long as the court is satisfied that the defendant was reckless as to *some physical harm* to some person, albeit of a minor character. As in all non-fatal offences where the *mens rea* includes recklessness, this is 'Cunningham' or 'subjective' recklessness — the prosecution must prove that the defendant did recognise the risk he or she was running.

Wounding or causing grievous bodily harm with intent (s.18)

This is a serious offence which carries a maximum sentence of life imprisonment (compare to s.20 with a maximum of 5 years). There are two forms of intent, the most common being 'with intent to cause grievous bodily harm'. This section requires proof that the defendant intended to cause a serious injury — 'specific intent' — see *R* v *Nedrick*, *R* v *Woollin*. This is either direct intent, where the defendant's aim or objective was to cause grievous bodily harm, or oblique intent, where the jury is satisfied that the defendant foresaw serious injury as virtually certain. In most cases of s.18 grievous bodily harm, the defendant will have used some form of weapon to inflict injuries on the victim, which makes it easier for the prosecution to prove the necessary intent. Where the prosecution fails to establish intention, the offence will be reduced to the lower s.20 offence so long as recklessness is proved.

Finished

Note that an alternative fault element is available for s.18, which relates to circumstances where a lawful arrest is being attempted and the intent is 'to prevent the lawful apprehension of any person'. The policy behind this element is that attacks on persons engaged in law enforcement are regarded as more serious. Under this head the defendant can be convicted if he or she pushes a police officer to prevent an arrest, and the officer falls and suffers a serious injury. There is no requirement that such serious results should have been foreseen or even foreseeable. It is, however, a requirement in such cases that the prosecution proves the defendant intended some harm, or was reckless as to whether harm was caused.

Summary of non-fatal offences

Crime	Actus reus	Mens rea	Cases	Maximum sentence
Assault	Causing the victim to apprehend immediate, unlawful personal violence	Intention or subjective reck-lessness to causing actus reus	Logdon, Ireland, Constanza	6 months or £5,000 fine
Battery	Infliction of unlawful personal violence	Intention or subjective reck-lessness as to inflicting unlawful personal violence	Fagan, Thomas	6 months or £5,000 fine
Section 47 ABH	Assault or battery causing actual bodily harm	Intention or reck-lessness as to the assault or battery	Miller, Chan-Fook, Savage, Parmenter, Roberts	5 years
Section 20 GBH/ wounding	Wounding: all layers of skin must be broken; GBH: serious injury	Intention or reck-lessness as to some harm	Eisenhower, Smith, Mowatt, Grimshaw	5 years
Section 18 GBH with intent	Wounding or GBH as in s.20	Specific intent to cause GBH, or intent to resist lawful arrest	Nedrick, Woollin	Life

Joint Charging Standard

The summary table below, agreed by police and the Crown Prosecution Service, has been produced in order to clarify the offences which would normally be charged following different levels of injuries. It is, however, important that you can also identify other potential offences which could be charged; for example, a minor cut or graze could potentially be charged as wounding.

Section 39 of the Criminal Justice Act: common assault (battery)	Section 47: assault occasioning ABH	Section 18 or Section 20: GBH or wounding
Grazes or scratches	Loss or breaking of tooth	Injury causing permanent disability or disfigurement
Abrasions	Temporary loss of consciousness	Broken limbs or bones
Minor bruising	Extensive or multiple bruising	Dislocated joints
Swellings	Displaced broken nose	Injuries causing substantial loss of blood
Reddening of the skin	Minor fractures	Injuries resulting in lengthy treatment
Superficial cuts	Minor cuts requiring stitches	
A black eye	Psychiatric injury — more than fear, distress or panic	

~··· Finish

Tort of negligence

This particular tort is by far the most important and most used tort in English law. The origin of the word 'tort' is Norman French, which came into our legal system after 1066, and it simply means a 'wrong'. A useful definition of tort is 'a wrong which entitles the injured party to claim compensation from the wrongdoer'. Another way of putting this is to say that someone is negligent if he or she acts carelessly towards another person, to whom there is a legal obligation to act carefully, and the carelessness causes the other person to suffer some harm or loss.

Winfield writes that 'tortious liability arises from the breach of a duty primarily fixed by law', and it is here that we need to start our study of the tort of negligence. The word 'negligence' is defined by the *Shorter Oxford Dictionary* as 'want of attention to what ought to be done or looked after; lack of proper care in doing something'. In law, negligence is more tightly defined as 'breach of a duty of care which causes foreseeable loss or injury'. To understand its application and importance it is necessary to study in turn each of the following three topics:

- duty of care
- breach of duty
- causation of foreseeable loss or injury

Duty of care

The tort of negligence owes its origins to the tale of a decomposing snail which was found in a ginger-beer bottle, probably the most famous single English case (although it was in fact a Scottish case) — *Donoghue* v *Stevenson* (1932). The facts are that the claimant, Miss McAllister (later Mrs Donoghue), went with a friend to a café where her friend bought her a bottle of ginger beer. Mrs Donoghue opened it and poured some of the contents into a glass. When she finished the glass, she then poured the remainder of the ginger beer into the glass and at this point the remains of a snail floated to the surface. This caused Mrs Donoghue to develop gastroenteritis and nervous shock, and quite naturally in these circumstances she sought compensation from the ginger-beer manufacturer. The case eventually reached the House of Lords, where Lord Atkin decided the case in her favour with his famous 'neighbour principle'. In summary, this stated that 'you must take reasonable care to avoid acts or omissions which foreseeably could injure your neighbour', who is in turn defined as 'persons who are so closely and directly affected by my act that I ought reasonably to have them in contemplation as being so affected when I am directing my mind to the acts or omissions'. In this case, the ginger-beer manufacturer should reasonably have had the claimant in mind when manufacturing and bottling his ginger beer.

This test clearly established that in order for a duty of care to be owed, there must be reasonable foresight of harm to persons who it is reasonable to foresee may be harmed by one's actions or omissions. Such 'duty' examples would obviously include cases involving doctor and patient, solicitor and client, car driver and other road users, employer and employee. However, the problem with this 'neighbour test' is that it has been used to create a duty of care in many less obvious situations, and the courts therefore have had to develop further guidelines to impose some limits on the scope of this principle. The modern approach comes from the case of *Caparo Industries plc* v *Dickman*, which laid down what is called 'the incremental approach'. This asks three questions:

- Was the damage or loss foreseeable?
- Is there sufficient proximity (a sufficiently close relationship) between the wrong-doer and the victim?
- Is it just and reasonable to impose a duty of care?

If the answer to all these questions is 'yes', then a duty of care has been established. This, of course, is only the start — the claimant also needs to establish that the defendant breached that duty of care and finally that the claimant's loss or injury was caused by the breach of duty and that such a loss was reasonably foreseeable (not too remote).

Foreseeability

The issue of foreseeability does not usually cause too much difficulty in the context of examination questions — it simply means that a reasonable person would have foreseen some damage or harm to the claimant at the time of the alleged negligence. A doctor's failure to diagnose a fairly common medical problem will foreseeably lead to complications; a car driver's mistake will foreseeably cause a road accident; a mining company which does not observe safety laws will foreseeably have employees injured in accidents, and so on. The case of *Langley* v *Dray* provides a clear illustration of this rule. Here, the claimant was a police officer who was injured in a crash while pursuing a defendant driving a stolen car. The Court of Appeal ruled that the defendant knew he was being pursued and therefore that by increasing his speed, he caused the police officer to drive faster and risk being injured.

Proximity

Proximity means closeness in terms of time, space or relationship, and in many cases the issues of proximity and that of foreseeability will be very similar; for example, in a road traffic accident the fact that the injured party could foreseeably be harmed will itself be proof of proximity. However, the case of *Bourhill* v *Young* is an interesting one in this context. The claimant was descending from a tram when she heard a motor accident. She did not actually see it but later saw blood on the road and suffered nervous shock and a miscarriage. Although it was reasonably foreseeable that some people would suffer harm as a result of the defendant's negligent driving, injury to the specific claimant was not foreseeable as she was not in the immediate vicinity of the accident — only hearing but not seeing the accident. Her action therefore failed.

Just and reasonable test

This final test is usually referred to as the 'policy test' under which judges are able to limit the extent of this tort. The principal reason for this judicial discretion is the argument that the floodgates would be opened if claims of liability were determined simply by reference to foreseeability. The American judge Cardozo CJ referred to this danger when he warned of 'liability in an indeterminate amount for an indeterminate time to an indeterminate class'. A good case to illustrate the use by courts of this discretion is *Mulcahy* v *Ministry of Defence*. In this case the defendant was a soldier who had served in the Gulf War where he had suffered damage to his hearing when a fellow soldier fired a howitzer shell. The Court of Appeal held that, although both factors of foreseeability and proximity were present, the facts of the case required them to consider this policy issue — effectively to ask whether it was fair, just and reasonable to impose a duty of care on the Ministry of Defence in battlefield situations. Unsurprisingly, it was decided that no such duty of care could be imposed. The application of this test can also be seen in the following types of cases:

- nervous shock — *Alcock* v *Chief Constable of South Yorkshire*
- pure economic loss — *Hedley Byrne* v *Heller*
- public organisations exercising a statutory duty — *X* v *Bedfordshire CC*

Breach of duty

Once the claimant has shown that the defendant owed him or her a duty of care, it is necessary to prove that the defendant breached this duty — in other words, it must then be proved that the defendant acted carelessly; for example, in *Donoghue* v *Stevenson*, that the defendant allowed the snail to get into the ginger-beer bottle. The key question that the court asks in order to determine whether this duty has been breached is: 'did the defendant behave as the reasonable man would have in these circumstances?' This test was described well by Baron Alderson in *Blythe* v *Birmingham Waterworks*: 'Negligence is the omission to do something which a reasonable man...would do, or doing something which a prudent and reasonable man would not do.' The standard is therefore an objective one — any personal difficulties or disabilities which might be encountered by the specific defendant cannot be taken into account. This is made clear in the case of *Nettleship* v *Weston*. Here the claimant gave the defendant driving lessons; on the third lesson, the car struck a lamp-post and the claimant was injured. It was decided that the defendant, although a learner driver, would be judged by the standard of the average competent driver: 'The learner driver may be doing his best, but his incompetent best is not good enough. He must drive in as good a manner as a driver of skill, experience and care.'

Tests to determine breach of duty

To assist the court in deciding whether the defendant has breached his or her duty of care, certain straightforward tests have been established. Each test is clearly illustrated by a case, and you therefore need to be familiar with both these rules and the accompanying cases.

Degree of probability that harm will be done

Care must be taken in respect of a risk where it is reasonably foreseeable that harm or injury may occur. Nearly all human actions or omissions involve the possibility of harm, but not every risky act will be regarded as negligent.

In *Bolton* v *Stone*, the claimant had been injured whilst standing on the road by a cricket ball struck over the defendant's ground. Evidence showed that a ball had only been hit out of the ground on six occasions in the previous 30 years, and on no previous occasion had anyone been injured. Here, the defendant was found not to have been negligent as a reasonable person would have been justified in disregarding the risk.

Compare this case with *Haley* v *London Electricity Board*. Here, the defendants left a hammer on the pavement to warn people of excavations. The claimant, who was blind, tripped over it and was injured. It was held that although the warning was sufficient for sighted people, it was not adequate for a blind person. The number of blind people was sufficiently large to make them a group which the defendants ought reasonably to have had in contemplation.

Magnitude of likely harm

The court considers not only the risk of any harm but how serious the injury could foreseeably be.

In *Paris* v *Stepney Borough Council*, the claimant, who had one eye, was employed as a mechanic in the defendants' garage where his job included welding. It was not normal to supply goggles and when a piece of metal flew into the claimant's good eye, he became completely blind. The defendants were held to be liable, although they would not have been liable to a person with normal sight. The greater risk to the claimant meant that greater precautions than normal had to be taken.

Cost and practicality of preventing the risk

Once the court has identified a risk as reasonably foreseeable, the next issue is whether the defendant should have taken precautions against that risk. If the cost of taking precautions to eliminate the risk is completely disproportionate to the extent of the risk itself, the defendant will not be held liable.

In *Latimer* v *AEC Ltd*, a factory was flooded, and the owner used sawdust to reduce the effects of the flooding. However, some areas of the factory floor remained slippery, and, as a result, an employee was injured when he fell. The owner was held not to have breached his duty of care because the only way to have avoided that risk was to have closed the factory completely. In the circumstances, this was out of proportion to the level of risk involved.

Note that *Bolton* v *Stone*, above, also illustrates this test effectively.

Potential benefits of the risk

In some cases, the court has to weigh up whether there are some risks that have potential benefits for society. In *Daborn* v *Bath Tramways* it was held that: 'If all trains were restricted to a speed of 5 mph, there would be fewer rail accidents, but our national life would be intolerably slowed down. The purpose to be served, if sufficiently important, justifies the assumption of abnormal risk.'

In *Watt* v *Hertfordshire County Council*, the claimant fireman was injured by a heavy jack which had been quickly loaded (but not secured) in the fire engine in order to respond to an emergency call involving a road accident victim. It was held that in these circumstances the risk involved was not so great as to prohibit an attempt to save life.

Professional persons

Where a particular defendant has a professional skill and the case involves the exercise of that skill, the court will expect the defendant to show that he or she has the degree of competence usually to be expected of an ordinary skilled member of that profession. This means that a general practitioner is only expected to exercise the normal level of skill of a GP, not that of a senior consultant heart surgeon. The leading cases here are both medical — *Bolam* v *Friern Barnet Hospital Management* and *Bolitho* v *City and Hackney Health Authority*.

In *Bolam*, it was held that 'a doctor is not guilty of negligence if he has acted in accordance with a practice accepted as proper by a responsible body of medical opinion skilled in that particular art'.

Causation of foreseeable loss or injury

The claimant must be able to prove both that his or her damage or injury was caused by the defendant's breach of duty and that the damage or injury was not remote, that is, it was reasonably foreseeable.

The first question that needs to be asked is the 'but for' question: but for the defendant's breach of duty, would the damage or injury have occurred? The leading case is

Barnett v *Chelsea and Kensington Hospital Management Committee.* The claimant's husband attended the defendants' hospital complaining of severe stomach pain and vomiting. The doctor in the Accident and Emergency department refused to examine him and he was sent home. Five hours later he died from arsenic poisoning. The defendants clearly owed the deceased a duty of care and equally clearly they were in breach by failing to examine him. However, they were held not liable because the facts established that, even if he had been examined, he would have died before diagnosis and treatment could have been carried out. As the deceased would have died regardless of the breach, the hospital was not the cause of his death.

In most examination questions this 'but for' test presents no problems, but it still needs to be addressed.

Remoteness of damage

Damages may not be awarded even where the claimant has established that the defendant's breach of duty (negligence) factually caused the damage or injury. It must be established that the damage was not too remote.

The present rule of law was laid down in the Privy Council case of *Overseas Tankship (UK) Ltd* v *Morts Dock and Engineering Co*. This is much better known as *The Wagon Mound No 1* case, after the name of the ship concerned. This case effectively overruled the case of *Re Polemis*, where it had been held that the defendant was liable for all direct consequences of the breach.

This test was held to be too wide and in the *Wagon Mound* case the present rule of reasonable foreseeability was laid down. The defendant negligently discharged fuel oil into Sydney harbour, and the oil spread to the claimant's wharf, where welding operations were taking place. The claimants were advised that there was no risk of this heavy oil catching fire on the water and as a result carried on welding. The oil did, however, ignite — sparks from a welder caused a pile of cotton waste floating on the water to catch fire, and this then set fire to the oil. As a result of this fire, damage was caused to two ships and fouling was caused to the wharf by the oil. On appeal, it was held that the defendants were only liable for the fouling to the wharf. The major damage to the ships caused by the ignition of the oil was too remote from the original discharge of the oil. The test for remoteness of damage was whether the kind of damage suffered by the claimant was reasonably foreseeable by the defendants at the time of the breach of duty.

The decision in this case was affirmed in the case of *Doughty* v *Turner Engineering*, which held that the defendant was not liable for the burns suffered by the claimant when an asbestos cover was accidentally dropped into some molten liquid. The resulting eruption of the liquid was too remote.

However, there are other rules which need to be learnt in addition to these. The first is that, if the kind of damage suffered is reasonably foreseeable, it does not matter that the damage actually occurred in an unforeseeable way. This principle is clearly illustrated by the case of *Hughes* v *Lord Advocate*, where the defendants had erected a tent over a manhole and surrounded the tent with paraffin lamps. The 10-year-old claimant dropped one of these lamps down the hole. Owing to an unusual combination of circumstances, there was an explosion and the claimant was badly burnt. Despite the defendants' argument that the explosion of the lamp was too remote, the House of Lords held they were liable. The question was asked: 'What kind of injury was foreseeable as a result of the breach of duty (leaving the hole unguarded)?' The answer was 'burns'. What kind of injury had occurred? Again the answer was 'burns'. The damage was therefore not too remote.

Another recent case which can be used to illustrate this rule is that of *Jolley* v *Sutton London Borough Council*. Here the claimant was a 14-year-old boy who had been seriously injured when he had tried to repair an old boat which he had found abandoned in a council park. While it was on a jack, the boat had fallen on him. The defendants admitted that the boat should have been removed from the park but denied liability for the accident, claiming that boys playing on the boat was foreseeable but the attempt to repair it was not. The Court of Appeal agreed with that argument, but the House of Lords reversed the decision — it was foreseeable that children would in some way 'get involved' with the boat. It was not necessary for the defendants to foresee the boy's attempt to repair it, using a jack to lift it.

'Thin skull' test

As noted on page 17, this states that, when the possibility of damage is foreseeable, the defendant must 'take his victim as he finds him' as regards physical characteristics. This means that the defendant will be liable when the injuries to the claimant are more serious than might have been anticipated because of factors peculiar to the victim.

The leading case which shows how this rule works in practice is *Smith* v *Leech Brain*. The claimant's husband was employed by the defendants. His work required him to lower articles into a tank containing molten metal. An accident occurred and Mr Smith was struck on the lip by a piece of molten metal. He later died of cancer which was triggered by the burn. Lord Parker CJ held: 'The test is not whether these defendants could reasonably have foreseen that a burn would cause cancer and that Mr Smith would die. The question is whether these defendants could reasonably foresee the type of injury which he suffered, namely the burn. What, in the particular case, is the amount of damage which he suffers as a result of that burn, depends on the characteristics and constitution of the victim.'

Damages

The purpose of damages is to put the claimant in the position he or she was in before the tortious act, as far as can be achieved by money. To calculate the award, damages are divided into two kinds — **special damages** and **general damages.**

Special damages

These comprise quantifiable financial losses up to the date of trial and are assessed separately from other awards, because the exact amount to be claimed is known at the time of the trial. The major heads of damages are:

Loss of earnings

This is calculated from the date of the tort to the trial.

Medical expenses

These cover any services, treatment or medical appliances, or the unpaid services of relatives or friends. Only such expenses as are considered reasonable by the court are recoverable. In *Cunningham* v *Harrison*, the claimant said he needed a housekeeper and two nurses to live in his home and look after him. The court refused to allow this claim as it was unreasonably large.

Expenses to cover special facilities

These can cover the cost of special living accommodation. The measure of damages here is the sum spent to obtain the special facility and its running costs — in *Povey* v *Rydal School* the claimant received an award to cover the cost of a special hydraulic lift to take a wheelchair in and out of a car. A large amount of money can be spent to adapt a house for people with particular disabilities.

General damages

This term covers all losses which are not capable of exact quantification, and they are further divided into **pecuniary** and **non-pecuniary** damages.

Pecuniary losses

The major head of pecuniary damages is future loss of earnings. The way in which courts approach this problem is to employ the notions of **multiplicand** (an annual sum to represent the claimant's annual net lost earnings) and **multiplier** — a notional figure which represents a number of years by which the multiplicand is to be multiplied in order to calculate the future losses. The multiplier is extremely arbitrary — it can never be precise and is calculated by looking at previous cases. Even in the case of a young wage earner, the maximum multiplier used is 18, because it is intended to take into account the possibility that the claimant may lose his or her job or retire early.

The expectation is that the claimant will invest any money received as a lump sum and use the income, and possibly some of the capital, to cover living expenses during the years when he or she would have been earning, so that by the time of retirement the whole of the sum awarded will be exhausted.

As victims of accidents often receive financial support from several sources in addition to tort damages — such as social security benefits, sick pay and private insurance — amounts are deducted from the damages award to account for these.

Other future losses

The claimant is entitled to an award to cover the cost of future care, such as nursing requirements and physiotherapy.

Non-pecuniary losses

The main heads of damages here are:

Pain and suffering

Compensation for pain and suffering is subjective as they are impossible to measure in terms of money. However, an award will be made to cover nervous shock and physical pain and suffering. It is important to achieve consistency between the awards made to different claimants who suffer similar injuries. The Judicial Studies Board sets 'tariffs' to govern the fixing of the appropriate figure. However, the tariff provides for a range of possible awards and a claimant who can show that the injury has had a particular impact upon his or her life may be able to recover at the high end of the range.

Loss of amenity

The claimant is entitled to damages for the inability to enjoy life in various ways, in particular impairment of the senses — this will include, for example, inability to run or walk, play sport or play a musical instrument. Such awards are assessed objectively and are thus independent of the victim's knowledge of his or her fate. In *West v Shephard* the claimant was 41 when she suffered a severe head injury. Although she could not speak, there was evidence from her eye movements that she understood her predicament, and so she received a high award for loss of amenity.

Damages for the injury itself

Injuries are itemised and particular sums are awarded for these on the basis of precedents.

Provisional damages

The general rule is that only one award of damages can be made. If damage turns out to be more serious than was anticipated at the time of the award, no further action is available to the claimant, and this can cause obvious hardship in personal injury cases. Under the terms of the **Supreme Court Act 1981 (s.32a)** the court has power to make a provisional award which allows the claimant to return to court should further anticipated serious deterioration occur. This power is not commonly used.

Structured settlements

These are not the result of legislation but of practical moves by lawyers and insurers to circumvent the usual lump-sum payments and increase the benefit to the claimant. In essence, they involve the substitution of pensions for lump-sum payments, and, because of tax concessions by the Inland Revenue, the result is lower payments by insurers and higher incomes for claimants.

Death of the victim

If the accident victim dies before being able to obtain damages, the victim's estate can bring a claim through legal representatives for all his or her losses prior to death — this could include pain and suffering, loss of amenity, loss of earnings and medical expenses. The victim's dependants can also claim under the **Fatal Accidents Act 1976**, which provides that a wide range of relatives may make a claim. To be successful, the relative must prove the fact of dependency on the deceased, which means the receipt of some benefit which can be measured in financial terms — earnings spent on the dependant, savings made for his or her future use, non-essential items such as holidays. In the case of *Spittle* v *Bunney*, the defendant's negligent driving had resulted in the death of the mother of a 3-year-old child. The child was awarded a 'ball-park' figure of £25,000.

Under the Fatal Accidents Act, the spouse of the deceased or the parents of a deceased, unmarried minor may make a claim for bereavement — this amount was increased from £7,500 to £10,000 in May 2002.

Sentencing

Before the judge imposes the sentence in a criminal case, a number of steps need to be taken.

Aims of sentencing

First of all, the judge has to consider which aims of sentencing are the most appropriate to the case. The main aims of sentencing are outlined below.

Retribution

This simply means punishment. As an objective of sentencing it is very simple — a person who has broken the rules shall be punished. It also includes the idea of 'just deserts' — an individual offender will receive a fair punishment which reflects both the seriousness of his or her offence and the moral fault of the offender. Every type of sentence, to a greater or lesser extent, can be regarded as a retributive one. The Court of Appeal, by using the 'tariff' system, gives judges much clearer guidelines as to the appropriate sentence in individual cases.

Deterrence

The purpose of deterrence sentencing is to deter offenders, and also other people, from committing crime. Individual deterrence aims to prevent the offender in question from reoffending, while general deterrence aims to deter others. A policy of pure deterrence would promote unpleasant sentences and, possibly, longer terms of imprisonment. It is clear from Home Office figures on recidivism (reoffending) that 70% of those offenders who receive custodial sentences go on to reoffend within 2 years of release, so this policy is not successful. With the present very low 'capture and conviction' rates, deterrence is most unlikely to reduce the amount of crime in general or the risk of an individual reoffending.

Reform or rehabilitation

This aim seeks to reform, treat or cure the 'criminal deviance' which caused the criminal to offend. It argues for resources being used to provide good educational and counselling services in prison and specialist units to treat sexual and drug offenders. It also favours the use of sentences designed to improve the offender's sense of self-worth.

Protection of society

This requires that serious offenders — especially those who have committed violent offences — should be imprisoned to protect other people. It is often called the 'prison works' idea. The **Criminal Justice Act 1991** laid considerable emphasis on this aim for serious violent offenders. In 2002 Lord Woolf CJ echoed this approach in the Court of Appeal when he called for mobile phone robbers to receive immediate custodial sentences.

Types of sentence

Having considered which aim(s) would be most appropriate in the case, the judge must then consider the types of sentence which are available. These fall into the broad categories outlined below.

Custodial sentence

This is the most serious form of sentence in English law — the deprivation of individual freedom by sending the offender to prison or to a Young Offenders Institution (depending on the age of the offender).

Section 79 of the **Powers of Criminal Courts (Sentencing) Act 2000** (PCCSA) provides that imprisonment is to be used only where such a sentence 'would be adequate to protect the public from serious harm' from the offender. Importantly, before the trial judge decides what length of sentence to impose in a particular case, he or she will seek guidance either from a Practice Statement from the Court of Appeal or from that court's consideration of a suitable 'tariff' for that kind of offence. The PCCSA also established the Sentencing Advisory Panel, which advises the Court of Appeal (under s.81) to amend its 'tariff' guidelines. In late 2002, the Court of Appeal responded to such a recommendation when it amended the tariff sentences for 'date rape'.

A custodial sentence may be suspended, which means that the offender does not go to prison unless he or she reoffends during the period for which the sentence was suspended. This may not be longer than 2 years. Suspended sentences are now very rare — s.118(4) of the PCCSA provides that they may be imposed only in exceptional circumstances.

Community sentence

Under the **Criminal Justice and Court Services Act 2000**, community rehabilitation orders (formerly probation orders), community punishment orders (formerly community service orders) or combination orders may be imposed. The court may place the defendant on probation for a period of between 6 months and 3 years. The defendant has to keep in touch with a probation officer, who helps the defendant to cope with housing, job and family issues and to address the crime committed. Such an order may include further requirements — for example, to attend a rehabilitation unit or to attend anger management courses. Community punishment orders involve from 40 to 240 hours of work in the community, supervised by probation officers.

Other community orders which can be imposed are curfew orders, drug treatment and testing orders, attendance centre orders (for under-21s), supervision orders (for under-18s) and action plan orders (also for under-18s).

Such sentences under s.35 of the 2000 Act can be passed only if the court is satisfied that the offence is 'serious enough' to warrant it.

Financial punishments

These are fines — a sum of money ordered to be paid by the offender to the Crown. This is by far the most common form of punishment and is most often imposed for motoring offences and minor 'either way' offences.

Discharges — absolute or conditional

Here the defendant is not sentenced as such, but if the discharge is conditional, he or she will be sentenced in respect of the original offence if another offence is committed within a specified period, which may not exceed 3 years.

Mitigating and aggravating factors

Before reaching a decision, the judge must consider both mitigating and aggravating factors.

Mitigating factors will be pleaded on behalf of the defendant by counsel and could include the following:
- this is a first conviction
- the defendant is a young offender
- a guilty plea was entered — this usually results in a one-third reduction in sentence
- the defendant has offered to compensate the victim

Aggravating factors are those which would normally result in a higher sentence being imposed, and include:
- the victim was especially vulnerable — either young or very old
- there was breach of trust
- the offence was committed while the defendant was on bail
- more than one defendant was involved
- there was use of a weapon

In 2002 the Lord Chief Justice announced a new Practice Direction, whereby Victim Impact Statements may be formally prepared and read to the court and the trial judge is obliged to have regard to these when considering the sentence to be imposed.

Maximum sentences

Finally, the trial judge has to understand what sentences are available for the offence committed. For assault or battery, the maximum is 6 months. For s.47 actual bodily harm, the maximum is 5 years. For s.20 grievous bodily harm or wounding, the maximum is 5 years. For s.18 grievous bodily harm with intent, the maximum is life imprisonment.

Questions
&
Answers

This section of the guide provides you with 11 questions which cover most of the Unit 3 topics. All of the questions are followed by A- and C-grade answers. After attempting them yourself, you should study the answers carefully — they provide an insight into the different techniques which these 'problem-solving' questions require. Remember the importance of using cases effectively — failure to use cases is one of the most significant differences between A- and C-grade answers.

For 'problem-solving' questions based on a short scenario, the mnemonic, **IDEA**, may help:

I   **Identify** the appropriate offence or tort element.
D   **Define** the specific offence or key element/rule of negligence.
E   **Explain** the various rules.
A   **Apply** the facts of the case to the rules explained, using **authorities** — both cases and statutes — to support your answers.

Examiner's comments

The candidate answers are accompanied by examiner's comments, preceded by the icon *e*. These explain the elements of the answers for which marks can be awarded, and are intended to give you an insight into what examiners are looking for. For A-grade answers, these comments show why high marks would be given. The comments given for C-grade answers point out the various weaknesses — lack of cases, inadequate explanation and irrelevant material, all of which cause marks to be lost.

To acquire the necessary skills and become more familiar with this style of examination question, it is a good idea to practise adapting these A-grade answers for different scenarios.

Question 1

Actus reus and *mens rea*

Explain the elements of *actus reus* and *mens rea* which in most crimes need to be proved to find the defendant guilty. (10 marks)

■ ■ ■

A-grade answer

Actus reus is the physical element necessary for a crime; it can consist of an act, an omission or a state of affairs. Actions could include attacking a victim or stealing. An omission or failure to act covers situations such as failing to wear a seat-belt or crash helmet (statutory duty), where the defendant has created a dangerous situation (*R* v *Miller*) or where the defendant has assumed a responsibility (*R* v *Stone and Dobinson*). An example of a state-of-affairs crime would be possession of a dangerous weapon or stolen property.

Mens rea is the mental element of a crime and consists of intention, recklessness — subjective (Cunningham) or objective (Caldwell) — or gross negligence. Intention can also be broken down into direct intention — aim, objective or purpose — and oblique intent where the court has to consider the related issues of probability and the defendant's subjective ability to foresee. The leading cases for oblique intent are those of *R* v *Nedrick* and *R* v *Woollin*, which both established the rule that (in a murder case) the jury can infer or find intent if it concludes that the defendant 'foresaw death or serious injury as virtually certain'.

 ✑ This is a clear and accurate answer, strengthened by good case references. The candidate demonstrates a sound understanding of both these elements and has covered in detail all the potential content of the mark scheme. This answer would receive 9 or 10 marks.

■ ■ ■

C-grade answer

Actus reus is the action part of a crime and *mens rea* means the guilty mind. An example of an *actus reus* would be attacking someone or stealing something; *mens rea* would be the defendant's intention, although sometimes it can be recklessness or even negligence. A good case of intention is *R* v *Hyam*, and for recklessness *R* v *Cunningham* where a man broke into a gas meter to steal money, and gas then leaked from the meter. An *actus reus* can also be an omission like not wearing a seat belt in a car.

 ✑ This is a weak and confused answer with no sound explanation of key material. The candidate is not able to explain the various types of *actus reus* — act, omission or state of affairs. The examples given — attacking or stealing — are superficial. No case examples are given for *actus reus*. *Mens rea* is also poorly explained, with no real detail given on either intention or recklessness. Negligence is wrong — it must be gross negligence. Although a case reference is given (*R* v *Hyam* should have been cited as *Hyam* v *DPP*), this case no longer represents the law. As for *R* v *Cunningham*, the candidate only gives a few facts about this case. The key legal point of this case is that it is the authority for subjective recklessness — the need to prove that the defendant foresaw a risk from his or her actions. This answer would receive 5 marks at best — a borderline grade C.

Strict liability offences

Some crimes are called strict liability crimes: using examples, explain why these crimes are so described.

(10 marks)

■ ■ ■

A-grade answer

These may be defined as offences which do not require *mens rea* to be proved — another way of describing them is to call them 'no fault' offences — and they are almost all created by statute law. Many concern road traffic offences or breaches of health and safety legislation.

A good example of such a crime is that of *R* v *Prince*, which involved the unlawful abduction of a 13-year-old girl. The jury found that there was reasonable evidence that she had told the defendant before the abduction that she was 18, and that he genuinely believed her. However, the court held that the relevant statute could be interpreted as allowing strict liability and that was all the act required for a conviction — the fact that the defendant did not know that she was under 16 was irrelevant as no *mens rea* for the offence was required.

The justification for strict liability crimes is that they are needed in the interest of public safety — to insist on proof of intention or recklessness in these cases would rarely produce a conviction. It is also argued that for most of such crimes the penalty is only a fine and that a conviction does not result in the defendant being stigmatised as a 'real' criminal.

   ☝ This answer has a good introduction which explains clearly that these offences are 'no fault' and then continues to identify fault with *mens rea*. Simple points are then made about these being mainly statutory offences, with accurate examples. The case of *R* v *Prince* is very useful, and its description is detailed. The final paragraph contains relevant material too. Overall, this answer would receive 7 or 8 marks. More case examples would have secured 10 marks.

■ ■ ■

C-grade answer

Strict liability crimes are things like speeding or parking where the prosecution is not required to prove intention. This means that a person can be convicted of a crime without realising it. Other examples of such crimes are pollution offences — see *Alphacell* v *Woodward*. Another case is *R* v *Larsonneur* where a French woman was convicted of being an unlawful alien in the UK despite having been forcibly put onto a ferry in Ireland. Usually, these crimes are punished by a fine so they are not serious.

   ☝ This is a weak answer in many ways. First of all, the candidate fails to define these crimes as 'no fault', which would have led to a discussion of *mens rea*. A particular weakness is the reference to conviction 'without realising it'. The examples given are acceptable but lack sufficient detail. The case of Larsonneur is not really appropriate as it is an example of an absolute liability crime. There is just enough material here for a grade C, but a maximum 5 marks would be awarded. If there had been any further omission or any factual inaccuracy the answer would be a grade D at best.

question 3

Crimes of omission

***Actus reus* will usually be a positive action; however, there are occasions where omissions (failures to act) can incur criminal liability. Explain how omissions can result in a crime being committed.** (10 marks)

■ ■ ■

A-grade answer

The general rule in English law is that an omission or failure to act will not usually result in criminal liability being imposed — there is no 'Good Samaritan' Law — but there are situations where a crime will have been committed because the defendant failed to act. These are as follows:

(1) Where there is a contractual duty to act — in *R* v *Pittwood*, the level-crossing gatekeeper failed to close the gate to an oncoming train and a person crossing the line was killed. His contract of employment clearly required him to ensure this could not happen. He was convicted of manslaughter.

(2) Statute can make it an offence in defined circumstances to fail to act — e.g. failing to wear a seat-belt or crash helmet.

(3) One can be made liable where there is an assumed responsibility for the care of an aged or infirm person — *R* v *Stone and Dobinson*. Here the defendants wanted Stone's middle-aged sister to live with them. This sister then 'assumed an eccentric, withdrawn and bed-ridden existence'.

(4) Where the defendant does an act which puts another person in peril or endangers that person's property or liberty, and the defendant is aware that he or she has created the danger, there is a duty to take reasonable steps to eliminate the danger. The act may be done without any kind of fault but, if the defendant fails to intervene, he or she is responsible. This is illustrated in the case of *R* v *Miller*, where a squatter accidentally set fire to his bed. He did nothing to put it out and went to sleep in another room. He was convicted of arson (deliberate fire-raising) — the judge ruled that when he woke up to discover the fire, he was under a duty to try to put it out, or at least to warn neighbours.

(5) Where an official fails to perform his duty — in *R* v *Dytham* a police officer was found guilty when he failed to protect a citizen who was being kicked to death. This would also deal with the hypothetical case of a life-guard who, having seen a bather in distress, failed to go to his or her rescue.

   🖉 This is an excellent answer in every respect. The candidate begins by noting that in general there is no liability for failing to act, and then describes in detail the exceptions whereby criminal liability is imposed for omissions. In the key areas, the relevant case is used effectively to illustrate the legal rule. This answer addresses all the potential content of the mark scheme, and would score 9 or 10 marks.

C-grade answer

Criminal omission is when the defendant fails to act — an example is in the case of
R v Miller where the defendant fell asleep while smoking a cigarette and then woke
up to discover the bed was smouldering, but rather than put it out or get help, he
went to sleep in another room. Miller was convicted of failing to act when he left the
fire to burn. Another type of omission concerns the responsibility to look after
members of a family — see *R v Stone and Dobinson*. A final situation is where a defendant has broken his contract of employment — there was a case involving a level-
crossing gatekeeper who failed to close the gate when a train approached and
someone was killed. The employee was convicted of manslaughter.

> The candidate has a weak grasp of relevant rules — there is no reference to the
> general rule on omissions, and the explanations and use of cases reveal a lack of
> detailed understanding, unlike the A-grade answer above. Only *R v Miller* is
> described adequately. This answer would be awarded 4–5 marks.

Coincidence of *actus reus* and *mens rea*

**Explain the legal rule which states that for a crime to be committed the
actus reus and *mens rea* must coincide.**
(10 marks)

■ ■ ■

A-grade answer

This means that the *mens rea* must occur at the same time as the *actus reus*. It is a major requirement for the imposition of criminal liability that the prosecution proves both the necessary *actus reus* and *mens rea*, but it must further be proved that these two elements coincided.

In most instances, this rule does not create problems, for example the attacker who strikes his victim with a broken glass or the murderer who kills his victim by shooting her with a shotgun, but there have been several real cases where this issue has been the central legal question which has to be resolved in order for the defendant to be committed.

The leading case example is that of *Thabo Meli* v *R* where the appellants attacked their victim intending to kill him; wrongly believing that the victim was dead, they pushed his body over a cliff to dispose of it. Medical evidence confirmed that the victim in fact died some hours later of exposure. The Judicial Committee of the Privy Council considered the defence argument that while the initial attack was accompanied by *mens rea*, that was not the actual cause of death, while the second act which was the cause of death was not accompanied by *mens rea*. However, in dismissing that argument, it was held here that 'it was impossible to divide up what was really one transaction'. The appellants' murder conviction was upheld.

This approach of 'continuing act' or 'linked transactions' was upheld in the manslaughter cases of *R* v *Church* and in *R* v *Le Brun*. A final case example is that of *Fagan* v *Metropolitan Police Commissioner*.

In conclusion, from the above cases, it can be seen that in the few instances where it has been argued as a defence that the *actus reus* and *mens rea* do not coincide, the courts have taken a robust and realistic line that, provided there is a series of 'linked transaction' or 'continuing act', it does not matter if the *actus reus* and *mens rea* do not 'precisely' coincide.

> *e* This is a comprehensive and well-argued answer. There is a clear introduction,
> which immediately establishes what this rule means. The candidate then takes one
> of the best illustrative cases and provides a sound factual explanation from which
> the legal rule can easily be ascertained. Further cases confirm the candidate's

detailed understanding of the 'continuing act' theory. This is confirmed again by a sound concluding paragraph. The answer would score full marks.

■ ■ ■

C-grade answer

If the *actus reus* and the *mens rea* don't coincide then the charge can be dropped altogether. The *actus reus* can usually be proved quite easily but the *mens rea* is more difficult because it means 'getting into the mind' of the offender, and trying to find out why he or she committed the offence. In a case called *Thabo Meli*, a gang beat up a victim intending to kill him, and they threw him over a cliff. The victim later died from exposure. Therefore, the defence argued that the men were not guilty as they did not have the *mens rea* when they threw him over the cliff, only during the beating. However, the judge found them to be guilty of murder, using what is known as the 'continuing act' theory.

This is a weak answer; the candidate gives a confused account of this rule from the beginning. Reference to how *actus reus* and *mens rea* can be proved is entirely irrelevant (and incorrect). Some marks are given for the case reference, where the facts are explained with reasonable accuracy and the 'continuing act' rule is identified, but not properly described. The answer would receive 4–5 marks.

Criminal law (1)

When John is drinking with friends in a pub, some youths start fighting among themselves. John approaches them and tries to stop them fighting. Dave, one of the gang, shouts at John: 'Mind your own business — if you want to interfere, I'll thump you.' Dave then lashes out at John and punches him twice in the face, causing serious bruising and a black eye.

Describe the *actus reus* and *mens rea* of two offences with which Dave could be charged as a result of John's injuries. (10 marks)

■ ■ ■

A-grade answer

The Joint Charging Standard agreed between the police and the Crown Prosecution Service would require the black eye to be charged as battery and the serious bruising to be charged under s.47 of the Offences Against the Person Act 1861, assault occasioning actual bodily harm (ABH).

Battery is defined as the intentional or reckless infliction of unlawful personal violence. Although there is strictly no need for any harm to be caused for this offence, in practice some minor harm is required to be proved. The black eye would be sufficient for the *actus reus* of battery. The *mens rea* is either intention or subjective (Cunningham) recklessness — conscious taking of an unjustified risk. Here, Dave deliberately struck John and this satisfies the *mens rea* of intention.

The *actus reus* of s.47 ABH is an assault or battery which causes actual bodily harm; ABH was described in *R* v *Miller* as 'any hurt or injury calculated to interfere with the comfort or health of the victim, provided it is more than transient or trifling'. The serious bruising to John's face would meet this definition. The *mens rea* for s.47 is the same as battery — this was confirmed by the cases of *R* v *Savage* and *R* v *Parmenter*, where the House of Lords held that for an s.47 conviction, the Crown does not need to prove that the defendant intended or was reckless as to inflicting ABH. All that is required is proof that the defendant intended or was reckless as to committing the offence of assault or battery — here it would be battery which has been described above.

> 🖉 In all such non-fatal offences, candidates are required to identify one or more appropriate offence. The easiest way to do this is to refer to the Joint Charging Standard, which is how this answer begins. While it is possible that assault and battery could have been chosen as the two offences, there are usually more marks available from citing the higher ranking offences. Here neither the bruising nor the black eye could be charged as either wounding (there is no cut in the layers of skin) or GBH, but could be charged under s.47 ABH. Both the *actus reus* and the *mens*

rea of each offence — battery and s.47 — are described clearly and accurately, and there is good use of case and statutory authorities. The candidate has also applied the rules of law to the facts of the scenario effectively. This answer would achieve 9 or 10 marks.

■ ■ ■

C-grade answer

According to the scenario, Dave shouted at John and then struck him twice, which resulted in bruising and a black eye. I think that Dave could be charged with both assault and battery, which are common-law offences. Assault is defined as intentionally or recklessly causing the victim to believe he or she is going to be attacked — here, by shouting at John, Dave could have caused John to think that he was about to be struck. It could also be assault, of course, if John saw the blows coming. Because Dave threw the punches deliberately, the *mens rea* of intention is present.

In the case of battery, this offence is committed when the defendant strikes the victim — there is no need for any level of injury to be inflicted. Here both the bruising and the black eye would be sufficient for the *actus reus* of battery.

The *mens rea* of battery is either intention to strike the victim or recklessness — in non-fatal offences recklessness is 'Cunningham' or subjective recklessness, which means that the defendant must have recognised that he or she was taking a risk.

  The candidate fails to refer to the Joint Charging Standard and has consequently fallen into the trap of selecting assault and battery instead of battery and ABH. This immediately limits the number of marks available. While both offences are described reasonably accurately in terms of *actus reus* and *mens rea*, the descriptions are thin, and only one case is referred to. This answer has just the minimum material for a grade C. It would score 4–5 marks.

6

Criminal law (II)

Richard and his girlfriend Alison had a serious argument at the end of which Alison, in her rage, picked up a kitchen knife and threw it at Richard. It struck him in the shoulder and caused a bad cut and damaged tendons.

With respect to the injuries suffered by Richard, Alison may be charged with an offence. Using examples, explain the *actus reus* and *mens rea* of an appropriate offence.

(10 marks)

■ ■ ■

A-grade answer

Given the cut to the shoulder and the damaged tendons, under the Joint Charging Standard, Alison would be liable to be charged under s.20 of the Offences Against the Person Act 1861. This offence is malicious wounding or inflicting grievous bodily harm (GBH).

The *actus reus* comprises wounding which is defined in *C (a minor)* v *Eisenhower* as a breach in the inner and outer layers of the skin, or grievous bodily harm, which was described in *DPP* v *Smith* as 'really serious harm' and in *R* v *Saunders* as 'serious harm'. The cut to Richard's shoulder would certainly qualify as a wound, and damaged tendons could be regarded as sufficiently serious to be GBH.

The *mens rea* of s.20 is intention or recklessness as to causing some harm, not necessarily wounding or GBH. This was laid down in the case of *R* v *Mowatt* and confirmed in *R* v *Grimshaw*. Recklessness here is 'Cunningham' or subjective recklessness — conscious taking of an unjustified risk.

While Alison may deny having intended to cause such injuries, her conduct was certainly reckless when she threw a kitchen knife at Richard. The prosecution would not find it too difficult to establish the necessary *mens rea* for s.20 in terms of the *Mowatt* direction.

Because the *actus reus* of the more serious offence — s.18 wounding or causing GBH with intent — is identical to that of s.20, it is possible for Alison to be charged with this offence. The only difference between the two offences is in the issue of *mens rea*. Section 18 is a specific intent offence — the prosecution must prove that the defendant intended to cause GBH. As Alison used a weapon this would be easier to prove. Intent here could be either direct intent or oblique intent, whereby the jury would have to believe that Alison foresaw serious injury as being 'virtually certain' in order to convict her under s.18.

> Note that this answer refers at the beginning to the Joint Charging Standard in order to identify correctly the most appropriate offence — s.20. Both the *actus reus* elements of wounding and GBH are defined correctly, using the relevant case

authorities. The *mens rea* is explained accurately too. Many students fail to note the *Mowatt/Grimshaw* rule about intent or recklessness as to causing some harm. The candidate then sensibly applies these rules to the facts of the scenario. It was not necessary to continue into s.18 GBH with intent, as this answer would already have received a high grade A, but the key point here is that if there is time to include material on s.18, it is worth doing so. The answer would score 9–10 marks.

■ ■ ■

C-grade answer

In this case, Alison could be charged with a number of offences according to her mental state and the harm caused to the victim, Richard. As a result of Alison's actions, Richard has suffered a bad cut and damaged tendons. Alison could be charged with ABH s.47 or even s.20 GBH under the Offences against the Person Act 1861. The test for this is subjective (Cunningham) recklessness. I have chosen s.20 as I think that this is a more suitable offence as regards Richard's injuries. Alison, by throwing the knife, has caused these serious injuries. GBH s.20 requires a good deal of *mens rea* – this can be intention or recklessness. Intent can be defined as direct which means the same as aim, objective or purpose, or oblique which was the case in *R* v *Hancock and Shankland* where striking miners killed a taxi-driver who was taking a strike-breaking miner to work. They gathered on a motorway bridge from which they threw rocks onto the motorway and a rock killed the taxi driver when it smashed through his windscreen.

Recklessness was defined in *R* v *Cunningham* which involved the defendant breaking into a gas meter to steal the money. This caused a gas leak which affected a woman upstairs. In this case, recklessness was defined as subjective — this means the defendant must have realised he was taking an unjustified risk. This test is difficult to prove.

The injuries suffered by Richard are certainly serious enough to be GBH — as there was also a deep cut, this could be wounding which requires blood to flow. The question does not indicate how bad the cut was, but strictly speaking any cut at all can be prosecuted as wounding — *R* v *Eisenhower*.

In my opinion, Alison would be convicted of this offence — she must have been reckless at least when she threw the knife at Richard, and it could even be called an intentional act.

> *ℓ* This answer demonstrates a number of the most common errors made by candidates who have not mastered the techniques required to answer a problem-solving question such as this. It is apparent from the opening paragraph that the candidate has not read the question set, which requires only one offence to be selected. Having chosen s.20, there is no attempt to justify this choice by providing legal definitions of either grievous bodily harm or wounding, nor is there any mention of the Joint Charging Standard.

The candidate then attempts to provide some explanation of *mens rea*, although writing that this offence 'requires a good deal of *mens rea*' is hardly convincing. As s.20 is a basic intent offence, references to oblique intent are irrelevant, particularly when an old case is selected rather than *Nedrick* or *Woollin* — there is also no reference to the elements of foreseeability and probability. The description of the case facts is entirely irrelevant. This is also the case with *Cunningham*. There is better treatment of the issue of wounding, although *Eisenhower* is cited incorrectly.

Finally, the conclusion is poor — candidates should never express a personal opinion as to the guilt or innocence of a defendant, as this is a matter for the jury to decide. This answer would score 5 marks out of 10 — just enough for a grade C.

Tort: duty of care

Fred is driving his car along a busy high street when his mobile phone rings. While reaching out for his phone he loses control of the car and crashes into a lamp-post. His passenger, Kate, suffers severe whiplash injuries. These injuries lead to a rare condition affecting the central nervous system, which causes Kate to experience partial paralysis to her left side.

The first test for the tort of negligence is whether a duty of care is owed to the claimant by the defendant. Explain whether in the above scenario Fred owes a duty of care to Kate. (10 marks)

■ ■ ■

A-grade answer

The issue of whether a duty of care was owed by Fred is the first test to be established in the determination of whether he is liable under the tort of negligence. The major case of *Donoghue* v *Stevenson* initially laid down the criteria for imposing a duty of care — this was the 'neighbour test' where Lord Atkin held that 'one must take reasonable care to avoid acts or omissions which you can reasonably foresee would be likely to injure your neighbour'. He proceeded to define a 'neighbour' as 'persons who are so closely and directly affected by my act that I ought reasonably to have them in contemplation as being so affected when I am directing my mind to the acts or omissions'.

From this principle, it can be seen that in order for a duty of care to be owed there must be reasonable foresight of harm to persons whom it is reasonable to foresee may be harmed by my acts or omissions. This rule was modified by the 'two-stage' test introduced in *Anns* v *Merton London Borough Council* which in turn was overruled in *Caparo Industries plc* v *Dickman*. This case laid down the present three questions which must be addressed in order for a duty of care to be imposed:

(1) Was damage or harm foreseeable?

(2) Is there sufficient proximity (close relationship) between the wrongdoer and the victim?

(3) Is it just and reasonable to impose a duty of care?

A good case to illustrate the issue of proximity is that of *Bourhill* v *Young*, where it was held that 'a duty of care only arises towards those individuals of whom it may reasonably be anticipated that they will be affected by the act which constitutes the alleged breach'. In that case, it was decided that the motorcyclist did not owe a duty of care to Mrs Bourhill, who at the time of the crash was standing behind a solid barrier and not within his field of vision, and was in no way at risk from his speed.

In this question, it can be argued that harm to Kate was foreseeable as a result of Fred's poor driving and that, unlike Mrs Bourhill, Kate was proximate to Fred because she was his passenger.

The final question — is it just and reasonable to impose a duty of care? — relates to the issue of policy. This question has arisen in the contexts of nervous shock, pure economic loss and statutory duties, where judges have taken on board the difficulties which might be caused were there no rules to limit potential liability. In the present case, there would appear to be no difficulty in holding that it is 'just and reasonable' to impose a duty of care on Fred, and indeed such cases of negligence are all too common in the courts today.

It may reasonably be concluded that on the facts provided in the scenario, Fred did owe a duty of care to Kate, on the basis of both the 'neighbour' and *Caparo* three-stage tests.

Most of the first part of this answer is given over to a full explanation of the relevant rules of duty of care, and only when these have been fully explained does the answer consider the circumstances of the scenario and apply the rules to the facts of the case. Note that with the exception of *Bourhill* v *Young*, none of the facts of the cases cited are described. These are two of the most common and serious weaknesses in examination answers. Many candidates answer such questions almost exclusively in terms of the facts of the scenario, and waste time describing the facts of cases, such as 'the snail in the bottle' case. Herein lies the main key to answering these 'problem-solving' questions. Most marks are given for a full and accurate explanation of the relevant legal rules — fewer marks are given to candidates who deal mainly with the facts of the case. The answer above has a clear structure related to the rules, starting with the 'neighbour principle' from *Donoghue* v *Stevenson*, then going on to *Caparo Industries plc* v *Dickman*. The issue of proximity needs more detailed discussion and here *Bourhill* v *Young* enables this matter to be clarified. Finally, the 'fair and reasonable' test is covered with good examples of 'policy' tests. This is a comprehensive answer which would receive full marks.

■ ■ ■

C-grade answer

In the modern law of tort the case of *Caparo Industries plc* v *Dickman* lays down the tests to be followed to deal with duty of care. This case has amended the rules laid down by *Donoghue* v *Stevenson* which concerned a lady who suffered stomach injury and nervous shock after she had consumed a glass of ginger beer into which a decomposing snail had dropped when she poured out the contents of the bottle. This case established the 'neighbour principle'.

Caparo laid down three questions which are asked to prove whether a duty of care was owed by the defendant to the claimant. These are: was harm or loss reasonably foreseeable, was there proximity between the claimant and the defendant (this means closeness), and is the claim fair and reasonable?

question

Here, Fred must owe Kate a duty of care because all road users owe a duty of care to other road users — as Kate was his passenger, she was close and proximate and some harm was foreseeable.

e While the facts of *Donoghue* v *Stevenson* are explained well, there is no explanation of what the 'neighbour principle' means. Although the three tests from *Caparo* are listed correctly, there is no real attempt to explain any of these in detail. Finally, the issue of application is addressed poorly. This answer would at best receive 5 marks.

Tort: breach of duty of care

Look again at the scenario outlined in **Question 7. Assuming that Fred did owe Kate a duty of care, discuss whether or not Fred was in breach of that duty of care.**

(10 marks)

■ ■ ■

A-grade answer

To decide this question, the traditional formula which the courts employ is to ask whether the defendant has observed the requisite standard of care in all the circumstances. The standard of care of 'the reasonable man' is what is usually expected. Failure to act as a reasonable person would have been an indication of negligence. This test is objective and requires a judge to measure the conduct of the defendant with that of the 'reasonable man' and what 'he' would have done in the circumstances. Alderson B. in *Blythe* v *Birmingham Waterworks* stated that 'negligence is the omission to do something which a reasonable man…would do, or doing some thing which a prudent and reasonable man would not do'.

There are a number of separate tests which provide some guidance as to how the 'reasonable man' question is to be decided — these are as follows:

- **The risk of harm** — in *Bolton* v *Stone* it was held that the defendant had not acted unreasonably in failing to guard against the remote risk involved — here evidence proved that a cricket ball had been hit out of the ground about six times in the previous 30 years. This case can be contrasted with *Haley* v *London Electricity Board*, where the defendants were held liable to pay damages to a blind person who had fallen into a hole, on the grounds that a large number of blind people live in London.
- **The magnitude of potential harm** — the leading case here is *Paris* v *Stepney Borough Council*, where the defendants were held to have been unreasonable in failing to supply safety goggles to a one-eyed workman who, when a chip of metal flew into his one good eye, was totally blinded.
- **The expense of taking precautions** — it would not be negligent to fail to take a precaution which is prohibitively expensive in the light of a risk which is not very great. In *Latimer* v *AEC* the factory owner was held not to have been negligent by covering slippery areas with sawdust. The only alternative would have been to close the factory. This extreme measure was held to have been unnecessary, and the claim failed.

To apply each of these tests in turn, first of all the risk and magnitude of harm: if a driver of a car allows his or her attention to slip, even for a moment, there is an obvious risk of harm, and in a road traffic accident there is always the potential for serious injuries or even death, especially to a passenger. It could also be argued that using a mobile phone while the car is in motion is a breach of the Highway Code, which would suggest breach of a duty of care. The final test, the cost of taking precautions, would seem to have little relevance here. It could therefore be strongly argued that Fred is in breach of his duty of care.

> This is another illustration of a very good approach to answering problem-solving questions. The answer concentrates on the relevant legal rules and then, at the end, applies these rules to the facts given in the scenario. There is an excellent introduction stating and explaining the 'reasonable man' test. The candidate then goes on to identify and explain the various tests which courts use to determine whether the defendant has acted as a reasonable person would in the same circumstances. In each of these, the relevant case authorities are used effectively to demonstrate a sound understanding of the rules. Finally, the candidate briefly but effectively applies these rules to the scenario. The answer would receive full marks.

■ ■ ■

C-grade answer

In breaching a duty of care Fred must have in some way been negligent — he cannot have behaved as a reasonable person would have. There are three tests to deal with this question. The first is the degree of risk, to see whether there is a high or low risk. This was what happened when a cricket ball was hit out of the ground and injured a person. It was decided that as it had only happened about six times in 30 years there was no breach of duty. The second test asks how serious the injury could be, and the final test is the cost of guarding against that risk — is the cost so high that precautions can't be taken?

To apply these tests to this situation, it seems obvious that Fred has not behaved as a reasonable motorist in trying to use the mobile phone while the car is in motion, and that the risk of injuring someone, possibly seriously, was quite high. Equally obvious, there was no cost involved in taking precautions — Fred should not have tried to answer his mobile phone.

> Compared to the A-grade answer above, the overall structure here is lacking in detail and case authorities. As so often, this C-grade answer provides evidence of only partial understanding. It would therefore receive just 5 marks.

Tort: causation and remoteness of damage

Look again at the scenario outlined in Question 7. Explain whether in this case Kate could recover damages for her injuries, particularly the damage to her central nervous system. (10 marks)

■ ■ ■

A-grade answer

The claimant, Kate, will not succeed in her action against Fred unless she can prove that his breach of duty was the cause of her whiplash and the further injury affecting her central nervous system. This question is a matter of fact and of law. Two factors have to be proved — these are:

(1) a causal link between the breach and the resulting loss or injury; and

(2) that the damage caused is not too remote from the negligent act.

The first of these questions has to be decided on the basis of factual causation, that is, the 'but for' test. Would the harm to the claimant have occurred but for the defendant's negligence? The key case to illustrate this is *Barnett* v *Chelsea and Kensington Hospital Management Committee*. In this case, it can be strongly argued that Fred's negligent driving caused the whiplash.

The second test — remoteness of damage — requires the claimant to show that the damage is, as a matter of law, not too remote from the original wrongful act. The decision in *Re Polemis* (liability for all direct consequences) was strongly criticised and effectively overruled in the later case of the Wagon Mound, which established the present rule of law whereby the defendant can be held liable only for the damage or loss which, as a reasonable person, he or she should have foreseen. If the damage or loss is too remote, the defendant is not liable. The decision in this case was affirmed in the case of *Doughty* v *Turner Engineering*. To apply this legal test here, Kate can surely maintain that the whiplash injury is a common consequence of a car accident and, as such, entirely foreseeable.

As regards the further medical problem of the damage to the central nervous system which has caused partial paralysis, this would be dealt with by reference to the 'thin skull' rule, which requires the defendant 'to take his victim as he finds him'. The leading case here is *Smith* v *Leech Brain*, where the claimant who had been burned in an industrial accident subsequently contracted cancer as a result of the burn and later died. Here, the defendant was held liable for both the original burn and the cancer. In this case, Kate should have little difficulty in recovering damages for both the whiplash and the subsequent paralysis.

💬 This is a well-planned and clearly structured answer which uses the material effectively. All the legal issues of causation, remoteness and the 'thin skull' rule are described fully, and effective use is made of leading cases. This answer would be awarded full marks.

■ ■ ■

C-grade answer

The remoteness of a loss relates to the issue of foreseeability of that loss or injury. The rule of law here was laid down in the case of the Wagon Mound, where a ship negligently discharged fuel oil into Sydney harbour; the oil slick spread across the harbour and was set alight by a welder — this caused damage to a ship, but, because it was unforeseeable that the oil would ignite in these circumstances, no liability was imposed for the damage to the ship. Here, the court would decide that the initial whiplash injury was a foreseeable consequence of Fred's poor driving and hold him liable to pay Kate compensation for this.

As for the more serious injury which caused some paralysis, Kate would probably be able to recover damages under the 'thin skull' rule, which means 'take your victim as you find him'.

💬 There is no reference to the issue of causation here, and the only case reference is to the Wagon Mound case. Unnecessary details are given about the facts of that case. If this answer had contained a reference to *Smith* v *Leech Brain* and/or to causation, it could almost certainly have gained a grade A, although no more than 6 or 7 marks out of 10 would be awarded here. As it stands, this answer would receive 4–5 marks.

Question 10

Damages

Look again at the scenario outlined in **Question 7. If Kate proved all the elements of the tort of negligence, she would be entitled to damages. Describe the methods used by the courts to assess the amount of damages to be awarded.**   (10 marks)

■ ■ ■

A-grade answer

The purpose of damages is, as far as money can do this, to put the claimant in the position he or she was in before the tortious act.

For purposes of calculating the award, damages are divided into two kinds — special and general damages.

(1) Special damages comprise quantifiable financial losses up to the date of trial and are assessed separately from other awards because the exact amount to be claimed is known at the time of the trial. They include:
- **Loss of earnings** from date of tort to trial.
- **Medical expenses** — any services or treatment. Only such expenses as are considered reasonable by the court are recoverable.
- **Expenses to cover special facilities** such as the cost of special living accommodation — the measure of damages here will be the sum spent to obtain the special facility and its running costs.

(2) General damages is a term that covers all losses which are not capable of exact quantification, and they are divided into pecuniary and non-pecuniary damages. The major head of pecuniary damages is that of future loss of earnings. This is calculated using the notions of multiplicand — an annual sum to represent the claimant's annual net lost earnings — and multiplier — a notional figure which represents a number of years by which the multiplicand is to be multiplied in order to calculate the future losses. Any social security benefits etc. will be deducted from the damages award.
Other future losses: the claimant is entitled to an award to cover the cost of future care — nursing requirements, physiotherapy etc.
Non-pecuniary losses: these include pain and suffering. Compensation for these is subjective as they are impossible to measure in terms of money.
Loss of amenity: the claimant is entitled to damages for the inability to enjoy life in various ways, in particular impairment of the senses — this will include, for example, inability to run or walk, to play sport or play a musical instrument.
Damages for the injury itself: injuries are itemised and particular sums are awarded for these on the basis of precedents.

e Note how this answer is laid out. It is structured clearly into the main sections or headings. This type of answer, with a number of separate points, lends itself to this kind of 'report-writing' style. For 10 marks, this is a very comprehensive and accurate answer covering all the main points of damages. Note also that there is no attempt to quantify the actual amount of damages that Kate might receive — indeed, Kate does not feature at all in this answer. Remember that quantification of the amount of damages is not included in this module — only the types or heads of damages.

■ ■ ■

C-grade answer

In deciding the amount of damages Kate would receive, the court would have to consider the type of damages she should receive. She may claim both special and general damages — special damages are those which can be costed up to the time of trial such as medical expenses. General damages are more difficult to deal with — the most important of these is future loss of earnings. Kate's injuries, especially the paralysis, might lead to her being unemployed for a considerable period of time, maybe even permanently, and so the judge will have to decide on a very large amount of money to compensate Kate.

Other types of damages include compensation for the injury itself — here, because Kate now suffers from paralysis, which is a serious condition, she would be awarded a great deal of compensation. Finally, she could receive money in respect of loss of amenity — loss of enjoyment of life.

e This answer has little structure to it when compared to the A-grade answer above. There is some knowledge of the various types of damages, but these are not explained adequately. The candidate makes the serious error of trying to personalise the answer as regards the claimant in the scenario, Kate. Nonetheless, this answer would receive 5 marks out of 10 — a bare C-grade pass.

Sentencing

Using the scenario in Question 5 about Dave and John, and assuming that Dave were to be convicted, outline the aims of sentence a judge would consider and explain the range of sentences which would be available to the judge. (10 marks)

■ ■ ■

A-grade answer

The main aims of sentencing are:

(1) Retribution: this simply means punishment. As an objective of sentencing it is very simple — that a person who has broken the rules shall be punished. However, it also includes the idea of 'just deserts'.

(2) Deterrence: individual deterrence aims to prevent the offender from reoffending; general deterrence aims to deter others.

(3) Reform or rehabilitation: this aim seeks to reform, treat or cure the 'criminal deviance' which caused the criminal to offend. Such an aim includes providing good educational and counselling services in prison.

(4) Protection of society: this, as its name suggests, requires that serious offenders (especially those who have committed violent offences) should be imprisoned. The Criminal Justice Act 1991 laid considerable emphasis on this aim for serious violent offenders.

There are a number of sentences that a court could impose on Dave. Sentences are of four types: custodial, community, financial and discharges.

- **Custodial sentences** are a term of imprisonment. This may be immediate or suspended, when the prison sentence is not activated unless the defendant commits further offences.

- **Community sentences** (now renamed under the Criminal Justice and Court Services Act 2000) comprise community punishment orders, where the offender has to perform a set number of hours of unpaid work from 40 to 240 over a 12-month period, and community rehabilitation orders, which place the offender under the supervision of a probation officer for a fixed period, between 6 months and 3 years. These two orders can be combined.

- **Financial sentences** are fines, which can be enforced through an attachment of earnings order. Compensation orders can be made for injuries caused or property damaged.

- **Discharges** may be absolute or conditional, the latter meaning that if the offender commits a further offence in the stated period, then the original offence may be resentenced.

In deciding the sentence, the court will look at aggravating factors (such as previous convictions) and mitigating circumstances (such as pleading guilty at the first opportunity, or provocation by the victim). In this case the unprovoked attack on an innocent stranger is likely to merit a harsh penalty, almost certainly imprisonment, because of the injuries inflicted. The maximum sentence for battery is 6 months, and for s.47 ABH it is 5 years.

> This is a comprehensive answer which would receive full marks. Both aspects of the question — aims and types of sentence — are explained clearly and accurately with appropriate use of statutory authority. The candidate has also referred to and described both aggravating and mitigating factors with good examples of each. Finally, the maximum sentences for each offence are stated correctly.

■ ■ ■

C-grade answer

If Dave were to be convicted of an offence, the courts might use a number of sentences available. One type of sentence would be a suspended sentence which means that if he reoffends within a given time, the original offence will be brought up again. He could also get probation or a community service order, or even both, which is called a combination order.

The most common type of sentence is a fine, but I think for Dave's offence this would not be sufficiently severe, and I would impose a prison sentence — this would deter him from reoffending and while in prison he could receive some form of counselling about alcohol.

> This is not a well-focused answer and it has limited factual content. The candidate has made the common mistake of trying to answer the question with regard to the specific offender mentioned in the scenario, instead of answering it as a general sentencing question. There are no marks whatsoever for suggesting a suitable sentence for Dave. The issue of 'aims' is dealt with only in passing in terms of the deterrent effect of a prison sentence, and the implied rehabilitative effect of alcohol counselling. The answer would score 4–5 marks.